A Special Educator's Perspective

YOUTH SUICIDE:
WHAT THE EDUCATOR
SHOULD KNOW

A Special Educator's Perspective

YOUTH SUICIDE:
WHAT THE EDUCATOR SHOULD KNOW

Eleanor C. Guetzloe
*University of South Florida
at St. Petersburg*

Foreword by Frank H. Wood

A product of the ERIC Clearinghouse on Handicapped and Gifted Children
Published by The Council for Exceptional Children

Library of Congress Cataloging-in-Publication Data

Guetzloe, Eleanor C.
    Youth suicide.

    "A product of the ERIC Clearinghouse on Handicapped and Gifted Children."
    Bibliography: p.
    1. Youth—United States—Suicidal behavior. 2. Suicide—United States—
Prevention. I. ERIC Clearinghouse on Handicapped and Gifted Children. II. Title.
HV6546.G825   1989   362.2   89–1312
ISBN 0–86586–188–9

A product of the ERIC Clearinghouse on Handicapped and Gifted Children

Published in 1989 by The Council for Exceptional Children, 1920 Association Drive,
Reston, Virginia 22091–1589.
Stock No. 331   Price $18.50

This publication was prepared with funding from the U.S. Department of Education,
Office of Educational Research and Improvement, contract no. RI88062007. Contractors
undertaking such projects under government sponsorship are encouraged to express
freely their judgment in professional and technical matters. Prior to publication the
manuscript was submitted to The Council for Exceptional Children for critical review
and determination of professional competence. This publication has met such
standards. Points of view, however, do not necessarily represent the official view or
opinions of either The Council for Exceptional Children or the Department of
Education.

Printed in the United States of America
10 9 8 7 6 5 4 3 2 1

Table of Contents

Foreword

In the view of the majority, the "healthy, normal view" shared by most of us, death is a shadow presence in the midst of life, a presence that is unwelcome and resented. Choosing the life we know, whatever its problems and pain, over the uncertainty of death, we guard ourselves and our loved ones as best we can against the change we know will inevitably come. The suicide of a fellow human being—friend or stranger—the seeming choice of early death over longer life—unbalances us. Why would anyone choose to invite death into our midst? With great reluctance do we admit that any conceivable explanation could be acceptable, and both religious organizations and the state have attempted to prevent suicide by establishing sanctions against it. The most general defense we adopt is to avoid discussing it or even thinking about it. Thus, if a suicide occurs we are caught by surprise.

As I was preparing this foreword, my attention was drawn to newspaper stories describing two different cases of adolescent suicide, each involving more than one death. In both cases, parents, friends, and teachers were asked by the reporters to explain what had occurred. In both instances, there was a familiar list of problems—conflicts with parents about the limits of independence to explore drugs, sex, music, and dress; conflicts with teachers about conformity to school standards; conflicts with peers about love, sex, and status. An involvement in "satanism," fostered by music and movies popular with today's adolescents, was also offered as a possible explanation in both cases. Yet, we all know that most young persons experiencing these problems and exposed to these same distasteful influences do not attempt suicide. The questions of "why this child" and "why this time" were not really answered in either case.

The suicide of a young person always seems particularly unnecessary to most of us. The suicide of a child or adolescent arouses in us a feeling that someone has failed in their responsibility to that young person. Young suicides are often referred to as "victims," and the genuine grief we parents, teachers, and friends feel at their deaths may almost be secondary to a disturbed sense of our own competence as caregivers. Our response is personalized. We turn back on ourselves, looking for ways in which our action or inaction may have contributed to an outcome so unacceptable.

Our sense of crisis is heightened by the knowledge that there is a contagion aspect to suicide. Once a group member has stepped across a boundary erected by social taboos, those who are vulnerable are drawn to imitate them. The unthinkable has become a dramatic topic for discussion. We must discuss suicide if we are to prevent it and respond to its occurrence. Yet, there is at least correlational data to suggest that public discussion and attention to suicide increases the probability of its reoccurrence. Whatever factors contribute to the "copycat suicide" phenomenon are especially strong during adolescence, affecting the group with which educators are especially concerned.

To write a book about this sensitive topic that may be read by parents and students as well as teachers, any author I would trust must combine compassion with clear thinking. Dr. Eleanor Guetzloe has these important qualities. She has not only studied carefully what others have written about suicide, but she has been in situations where she experienced at first hand the anguish of persons at risk for self-injury or death and the grief and soul-searching of survivors. These personal experiences have deepened her sense of compassion but have not taken from her the ability to think clearly about the best responses we can make to prevent the occurrence of suicide and to restore social equilibrium when it has occurred. Her approach may be described as honest in facing the facts, cautious in putting forth answers or explanations, and positive in suggesting steps for prevention.

Some people who read this book will be under pressure to act immediately to prevent or respond to suicide. They will be tempted to dash ahead to the "how to" prevent or repair sections of the book without reading Dr. Guetzloe's carefully prepared lessons presenting what is known about the social dynamics of suicide. This would be a mistake. We need to learn as much as we can of the well established knowledge about suicide and its causes, while recognizing the vast amount that is not known, before we seek to act. The reader should remember that Dr. Guetzloe is not more interested in talking about problems than taking action against them. She has researched the literature on suicide because she is concerned that our actions be informed by knowledge. In responding to suicide, we cannot afford to repeat avoidable mistakes others have made.

Dr. Guetzloe alerts us to symptoms of suicidal tendency in individuals and shares plans for response based on the experiences of those working in crisis centers. But, she makes it clear that our best efforts in times of crisis are sometimes cases of too little, too late.

Major efforts must also be addressed to prevention. The best way to respond to suicide is to promote healthy satisfaction in living so that the thought of prematurely ending the experience remains remote for us. Dr. Guetzloe suggests life-enhancing activities that can help inoculate groups and individuals against suicide.

Dr. Guetzloe gives us a well written, hopeful book that will provide support and guidance to educators wishing to help our young people grow up valuing and cherishing the fragile gift called life.

Frank H. Wood
Professor, Special Education Programs
University of Minnesota

Minneapolis, Minnesota

Acknowledgments

To the research librarians at the University of South Florida at St. Petersburg, who often knew my needs before even I did;

    To Mercedes Anderson, my dear friend, who set aside her own tasks to help with the first round of typing;

    To Sue Blanchard, my doctoral student, who created the first draft of a reference list from my little pieces of paper and cardboard;

    To Bill Rhodes, my treasured friend and colleague, for the first review of the manuscript;

    To June Jordan, Editor in Chief of CEC Publications, for her patience and understanding;

    To the many individuals who furnished a wealth of information by mail or telephone; and

    To my family, for tolerating the incredible pile of paper that they came to call, "Suicide, She Wrote,"

    I would like to express my eternal gratitude.

About the Author

Eleanor Carden Guetzloe, Ed.D., is a Professor in the Department of Special Education, University of South Florida, St. Petersburg. She has been a classroom teacher in Hillsborough County, Florida, Public Schools and a demonstration class teacher and Director of the On-Campus Clinic for Emotionally Disturbed Children, University of South Florida.

In 1979 when Dr. Guetzloe began studying suicide, she saw it as education's responsibility.

> We have to make school a place where children will want to be so they don't drop out and they don't kill themselves. A negative school environment can be devastating to a child—and he's forced to be there. We have compulsory education, but we're not mandated to make school a positive place.

This book is a result of Dr. Guetzloe's belief that everyone is affected by youth suicide and that to solve the problem, a "total effort" is needed—"It's a total effort—parents, the community, and all the people in the schools, from cafeteria workers, to bus drivers to security officers. If these folks would all stay in touch, then children would have less of a chance of falling through the cracks."

Dr. Guetzloe is a member of The Council for Exceptional Children and its Division, the Council for Children with Behavioral Disorders. She is now Vice President of the CCBD Division and will serve as President in 1991–1992.

PART I
Toward an
Understanding of
Youth Suicide

1. Introduction

Within the last three decades, the suicidal behavior of children and youth—formerly considered to be the responsibility of mental health professionals—has become a serious concern of teachers, administrators, and other school personnel. In many districts across the continent, educators are now involved in promulgating plans for prevention programs that are appropriate for the school setting. There is a serious need for information regarding the school's responsibility in helping to prevent this tragic phenomenon.

THE PURPOSE OF THIS BOOK

In discussing his own work, Maris asked, "But why another book on suicide? Suppose we grant that suicide and death are interesting and important topics, even fundamental human concerns. Has not enough been written already?" (1981, p. 3). Maris's own response was that he and his associates hoped that what had already been said could be said better, integrated, and made clearer.

That is the purpose of this book. It has been written primarily for educators, from a special educator's point of view. It is an attempt to provide current, accurate, and practical information that would be useful to all educators in (a) understanding the phenomenon of suicidal behavior and (b) developing programs for intervention within the school setting. The text includes neither the many discussions on theory or philosophy that can be found elsewhere nor information that is clearly intended for another audience. The reference list is extensive, because I believe that authors have a responsibility to document their sources (particularly regarding sensitive topics). Further, even more important than the information that is included is the information that is not. Like Diogenes in search of an honest man, I have searched for truth (often in the middle of the night).

Writing a book on youth suicide is a tremendous responsibility— neither easy nor to be taken lightly. Selecting suitable material from the enormous body of literature was a time-consuming task, but the primary cause of many sleepness nights (and recurring writer's paralysis) was the understanding that inaccurate information could be harmful to children.

SOURCES OF INFORMATION

The information included in this text has been derived from three major sources—the literature (national and international journals, books, government reports, newspapers, bulletins, newsletters, and magazines), the media (television, films, and radio), and personal experiences (contacts with psychiatrists, psychologists, social workers, counselors, teachers, administrators, parents, students, suicidal individuals, and strangers). No reliable source has been omitted. In discussions with professionals, parents, and students; in meetings of committees and task forces engaged in planning and implementing suicide prevention programs; during lectures and workshops for professionals from a variety of disciplines; and in conversations with suicidal young people, I have not only taught, but also learned.

WHY SHOULD A SPECIAL EDUCATOR BE INTERESTED IN SUICIDE?

My personal interest in suicide prevention (and eventually this book) grew out of a suicide crisis of an adult more than 8 years ago. Early one morning, my husband asked me to come quickly to the local marina to counsel a friend, who had rigged his cabin cruiser to explode (along with himself and the marina). Divorced from his wife of many years, he had been living with a younger woman, and she had just left him for another man. Feeling woefully inadequate, I went aboard and spent 2 hours with our friend, exploring other alternatives to his killing himself. In some desperation, I finally suggested that he should, at least, remove her name from his personal and business bank accounts before continuing with his plan, so that she would not profit from his demise. Revenge was a powerful motivator; he came off the boat, went to the bank, and chose to live. He still does.

During the following week, I told my graduate students about this experience. I was made aware that almost every one of these people, who were special education teachers, counselors, or administrators in a variety of settings, had been personally touched by suicidal behavior—generally of their students. Among the exceptional student population, suicidal behavior was apparently a tremendous (and often unreported) problem. Until then, I had included the topic of suicide, along with substance abuse and running away, as part of one evening's lecture in a graduate course on the adolescent exceptional student. This was obviously not sufficient.

As occasionally behooves a college professor, I conducted a computer search of the literature, finding literally thousands of citations on the topic of suicide but comparatively few related to suicide among children and adolescents. There was also a paucity of data related to suicidal behavior among exceptional children, with the exception of those that would be categorized as seriously emotionally disturbed. The information that was available dealt primarily with risk factors associated with suicide; very little was written about appropriate intervention. Most obvious of all, to an educator, was the apparent tendency of many authorities to ignore the importance of the educational system—as part of either the solution or the problem. Authors often called for public education programs for teaching the warning signs of suicide, but educators were rarely included in lists of potential rescuers. Many times the only intervention suggested for educators was to refer suicidal children to mental health professionals for assistance. This should be good advice; but (a) educators usually cannot refer a child to an agency outside the school without prior parent permission, (b) the parents may be reluctant to seek professional help, (c) the number of trained mental health professionals has not kept pace with the need, and (d) the effectiveness of traditional treatment is subject to question. It was (and is) my opinion that the school should assume a greater responsibility in preventing this tragedy, but school professionals need a great deal of information and training to plan appropriately for school intervention.

A CONTROVERSIAL ISSUE

The establishment of suicide prevention programs in the school, as well as the topic of suicide itself, is still controversial. While some authorities argue for massive public awareness campaigns, others point to the possibility of contagion that may result from increased interest in the topic. Basing an opinion on information that seems to be reliable, I have attempted to present a comprehensive but cautious approach for school personnel to follow in planning and implementing school-based programs for suicide prevention.

The preference for a cautious approach is based on the following understandings, gleaned from both the literature and personal experience:

1. In the great bulk of information on the topic of youth suicide, there is a relative paucity of findings from well-designed studies. Many articles have been based on author opinion, intuition, thoughts, and feelings, rather than on empirical data. Sometimes these "clinical hunches" have been confirmed by studies conducted at a later time. In other instances, findings of recent studies have refuted the claims of earlier writers. Every attempt has been made to include only accurate information from the literature, whether originally data based or confirmed by later research.

2. There are no data available to support the effectiveness of suicide prevention programs in the schools. On the other hand, there are data from recent studies on risk factors and contagion that indicate a need for caution in planning for such programs. The problem of youth suicide is not the same as a problem in reading, mathematics, science, or social studies. A reading program that is unsuitable for an individual child might delay learning, but an inappropriate instructional program on the topic of suicide could be lethal.

3. There are many individuals who have "jumped on the youth suicide bandwagon," claiming to be knowledgeable in this area. Youth suicide is a topic of considerable current interest, and there has been a veritable proliferation of not only literature and media but also instant "experts" that may be more harmful than helpful. Educators who are involved in planning or implementing suicide prevention programs need to be able to discriminate between those individuals, activities, and materials that are appropriate for children and those that may actually be dangerous. The suggestions in this text are both positive and safe.

4. An appropriate and effective suicide prevention program for any school or district should be developed by the members of that community and should reflect both the needs of their students and the resources that are available. Educators should be extremely wary of commercially available programs. Many of these were planned for a specific school district; some have been hastily thrown together for quick marketing; and very few have been subjected to any kind of evaluation. Some were not even effective in the communities for which they were designed, if a reduction in the rate of suicide is a criterion. This text includes suggestions for educators to follow in planning and implementing their own "school-friendly" program.

A PRACTICAL APPROACH FOR EDUCATORS

The suggestions presented in this text have come from a practical "If . . . then" approach, which is a special educator's orientation. If a certain risk factor is related to suicidal behavior, then intervention related to that problem should prove to be preventive. Many problems associated with youth suicide are school related and remediable; they lie in teachable areas and can be addressed in the school—in policy, procedures, and curriculum. If the problem is beyond the limits of school intervention, then another agency's assistance must be procured; but school personnel can help to carry out the appropriate interventions.

A SHARED RESPONSIBILITY

Suicide prevention is not the responsibility of the school alone. Children function in several spheres—in the family, in the school, and in the community—and each of these institutions shares the responsibility for preventing suicidal behavior in children and youth. Although school intervention is now mandated in many districts, an effective suicide prevention program must provide for the cooperation of all who come in contact with a child in distress. The school, however, can assume the responsibility for leadership in this regard.

ORGANIZATION OF THE TEXT

This book is organized in two major sections. Part I addresses background information on suicide that should be helpful to educators in understanding this problem. Part II provides suggestions for developing school-based suicide prevention programs.

The suicide incidents described in the text have been depersonalized to whatever extent possible, in an effort to avoid bringing further pain to the family or friends of the children involved. These cases were either reported in the media or related by individuals who were knowledgeable about the child in question—family, friends, teachers, counselors, therapists, and law enforcement agents.

Any occasional references to a suicidal child as "he" or "him" are not intended to be sexist or discriminatory, but are rather for the purpose of making the text more readable. For purposes of this discussion, occasional references to the male gender are considered to be generic. It is clearly understood that suicide is no respecter of race, religion, nationality, intelligence, social class, financial standing, or sex.

2. The Study and Prevention of Suicide: A Brief History

Suicide has been part of history for as long as there have been written records and is probably as ancient as mankind. The first known document about suicide is an Egyptian record, written on papyrus, that historians believe was written between 2000 and 1900 B.C. (Williams, cited in Allen, 1977). From that time to the present, suicide has been a topic of considerable interest to many authors from a variety of disciplines.

Allen (1977) has outlined the history and background of suicidology from the earliest recorded documents to the mid-1970s. Numerous other authorities have also provided historical perspectives on this topic, including Alvarez (1972, 1975), Dublin and Bunzel (1933), Rosen (1975), and Shneidman (1973a, 1973b). Dublin's contributions have been recognized as particularly important by suicidologists; his first book (Dublin & Bunzel, 1933) has been called "The Encyclopedia Britannica of Suicide" (Shneidman, 1970a).

EARLY STATISTICS ON SUICIDE

John Graunt, a London tradesman, systematically organized information from the London bills of mortality into separate categories and published the first mortality tables in 1662 (Shneidman, 1973). In 1741, Johann Peter Sussmilch, a Prussian clergyman, began keeping vital statistics by analyzing data from church records (Allen, 1977). Research on suicide that included statistical information was first reported in the early 19th century (Allen, 1977). In Esquirol's *Des Maladies Mentales (Mental Maladies: A Treatise on Insanity)*, which was published in 1838, the section on suicide included both case studies and statistical tables. By the middle of the 19th century, most European countries were publishing suicide rates (Lewis, 1956). Suicide, along with murder, prostitution, alcoholism, and other crimes, was classified under the general category of moral statistics. As these phenomena were perceived as morally problematic, the moral statisticians used their data as a quantitative index of the moral health of a society. With the accumulation of statistics, it became apparent that there were significant variations in the suicide rates of countries or geographical areas and that these rates remained quite consistent over time.

In 1897, Emile Durkheim published the first edition of *Le Suicide*, one of the best known and highly regarded studies of suicide. It is still considered to be a model for the use of the statistical method in social investigation (Simpson, 1951; S. Taylor, 1982). Durkheim's three major etiological categories—egoistic, altruistic, and anomic—are widely quoted and have had a considerable impact on the study of causal factors. The study, however, focused on adult suicide, with little mention of the suicides of people under the age of 20.

According to Durkheim, suicide results from society's having either too much or too little control over the individual. Egoistic suicide occurs when an individual feels alienated and has too few ties to society or community. This category would include the suicide of a lonely, unmarried, and unemployed person or that of a runaway child who is alone and friendless. Altruistic suicide would be dictated by custom or rules of society. It occurs among people who are so dedicated to a cause that duty is more important than life. Examples would be the cases of Japanese kamikaze pilots or, more recently, the suicides of members of a religious cult (Wellisch & Ungerleider, 1985). Anomic suicides would result from a sudden and great change in the relationship between the individual and society. This type of suicide would be precipitated by a person's becoming bankrupt, losing a job, being divorced, or ending a love affair. Anomie, according to Durkheim, occurs in societies in which social institutions have changed so quickly that people feel confused about their positions and goals, with rapid changes bringing great unrest.

Durkheim described a fourth category—fatalistic suicide—only in a footnote. Fatalistic suicide occurs when a person apparently has no reasonable or acceptable alternative, such as the suicide of a prisoner who is being tortured and expects to be killed by his captors or that of a terminal cancer patient who kills himself to end the pain.

Since the publication of Durkheim's study, a great number of articles and books have been written on the topic of suicide. Farberow (1969) compiled a bibliography of approximately 3,500 works on this subject that had been published between 1897 and 1967, and there has been even greater proliferation in the past 20 years. The current high level of interest in the prevention of suicide, however, is a relatively recent development (Dublin, 1969).

HISTORY OF SUICIDE PREVENTION

Early in the 20th century, interest in suicide prevention was generally confined to theoretical and philosophical considerations among psychiatrists, lawyers, and the clergy, and the prevailing attitude was that there was little, if any, hope for either controlling or preventing this phenomenon (Dublin, 1969). Among those who made efforts to assist suicidal individuals were "a few brave spirits who, without special learning or skills, were moved by simple compassion for those in distress and . . . made efforts to save them" (p. 44). Among these brave souls were representatives of churches and other groups such as the Salvation Army in England, Germany, and the United States.

Suicide Prevention Services and Agencies

The first suicide prevention service in the United States was established in 1905 in New York City by a Baptist minister, Harry Warren. First called The Parish of All Strangers, its name was changed in 1906 to The National Save-A-Life League. Also in 1906, the Salvation Army in England established a suicide prevention bureau, the London Anti-Suicide Department. In 1933, a squadron of boats from Budapest, Hungary, patrolled the Danube River to rescue potential suicides. In 1947, the Society for the Care of People Tired of Life was founded by Dr. Edwin Ringel in Vienna, Austria.

The Samaritans were established in Britain in the mid-1950s by the Reverend Chad Varah, for the expressed purpose of "befriending" people who were desperate or suicidal (Varah, 1966). This nonsectarian group became the model for a worldwide organization which is now also in existence in communities across the North American continent. Then in Boston in 1959, Catholic Father Kenneth Murphy established Rescue, Incorporated, a church-sponsored suicide prevention service.

These early suicide prevention agencies, and other similar organizations that followed, generally served adult populations, people who were capable of self-referral. Relying primarily on both professional and nonprofessional volunteers, the agencies arranged personal interviews, provided basic psychotherapy, and referred suicidal individuals to mental health professionals for further treatment.

The Los Angeles Suicide Prevention Center. A milestone in suicide prevention in the United States was the establishment of the Los Angeles Suicide Prevention Center in 1958 by Drs. Edwin Shneidman and Norman Farberow, funded by a research grant from the National Institute of Mental Health. The center quickly became a model throughout the country for research and training as well as for the provision of services to suicidal individuals.

The NIMH Center for the Studies of Suicide Prevention. In 1966, the National Institute of Mental Health (NIMH) established the Center for the Studies of Suicide Prevention with an overall goal of lowering the rate of suicide through research and training and encouraging the growth of suicide prevention efforts throughout the United States. The establishment of this center provided the impetus for the development of other suicide prevention programs. Most of the over 200 suicide prevention programs in this country have been organized since that time (Hendin, 1982).

The National Mental Health Association. The National Mental Health Association has provided a great deal of assistance in promoting the development of suicide prevention centers in the United States. According to Hendin (1982), a community mental health association was often the major stimulus for the establishment of a local suicide prevention agency. Support from local mental health associations may include leadership for the development of the program, ongoing financial assistance, and continued involvement in the program administration.

Associations for Suicide Prevention. In 1961, the International Association for Suicide Prevention, with headquarters in Vienna, Austria, was founded by Dr. Edwin Ringel. In 1967, Dr. Edwin Shneidman founded the American Association of Suicidology for the purposes of the study and prevention of suicide. In that year, the first edition of the *Bulletin of Suicidology* was published.

Formal Study in Suicidology. The first formal postgraduate Fellowship Program in Suicidology was offered by the Department of Psychiatry and Behavioral Sciences at the Johns Hopkins University School of Medicine in 1967. The program emphasized three areas: suicide research, crisis theory and intervention, and mental health sciences including community psychiatry (Perlin, 1975).

STUDY OF YOUTH SUICIDE

The first descriptions of suicidal children appeared in French and German psychiatric journals in the late 19th century (Pfeffer, 1986). Most of the early discussions of suicidal behavior in children and adolescents were presented by psychoanalysts. As a result, many hypotheses about youth suicide have been formulated on the basis of psychoanalytic theory.

In 1910, following an increase in suicide among the young, a symposium entitled "On Suicide, with Particular Reference to Suicide Among Young People" was held by a group of psychoanalysts in Vienna, Austria. The major focus of the symposium was on the role of education in both causing and preventing youth suicide. For purposes of this discussion, education included learning, pedagogy, acculturation, and environment (Shneidman, 1969). Among the topics discussed at the symposium were school failure, family constellation, desire for revenge, unrequited love, discrepancy between ability and achievement, parental pressure, and the influence of mass media and publicity on suicide contagion and imitation (Friedman, 1967). In the opening presentation, David Ernst Oppenheim cited Prussian statistics that (a) indicated an increase in the suicide rate for young people of from 7.02 per 100,000 in 1883 to 8.26 per 100,000 in 1905 and (b) defended the school against the charge of causing the increase (Friedman, 1967).

Sigmund Freud also spoke at the symposium, making the following remarks related to the role of the school:

> A secondary school should achieve more than just not driving its pupils to suicide. It should give them a desire to live and should offer them support and backing at a time of life at which the conditions of their development compel them to relax their ties with their parental home and their family. It seems to me indisputable that the schools fail in this, and in many respects fall short in their duty of providing a substitute for the family and of arousing interest in life and the world outside. (cited in Havighurst, 1969, p. 63)

Research on Youth Suicide. According to Friedman (1969), the 1910 symposium became a blueprint for the next half century of research on youth suicide. Though the subject had not been unstudied before then, most of the previous investigations had focused on suicide among adults.

In the last 20 years, there has been a considerable increase in research and other writing activity related to youth suicide. Seiden

(1969) compiled a bibliography of more than 200 books and articles on the topic of youth suicide that were published from 1900 to 1967. Between 1967 and 1977, there were at least 275 more (Pardes, 1985). There are now thousands of references to youth suicide in the literature. The focus, however, has changed over the years from lamenting the problem to considerations for intervention and prevention.

> Study of suicide begun during the early part of this century has evolved into study of its prevention. Authorities from a number of widely varying disciplines are contributing to man's knowledge on suicide. Research continues along avenues seemingly far apart. But their goals are essentially the same: to save lives and to improve mental health. (Shneidman & Mandelkorn, 1970, p. 137)

Current issues related to the study and prevention of youth suicide are discussed in the next chapter.

3. Current Trends and Issues Related to Youth Suicide

Within the last decade, youth suicide has become a major social, medical, and educational problem in the United States, Canada, and other countries around the world. In response to the growing public concern, steps have been taken by a variety of public and private groups to provide information about the problem of youth suicide and to establish programs aimed at prevention. In the United States, a national committee composed of representatives from every state was established for purposes of increasing public awareness, securing funding for research and intervention, and providing a clearinghouse on effective programs (Tugend, 1984b). The National Institute of Mental Health (NIMH) funded a number of research studies to investigate youth suicide in addition to those normally conducted by the Institute itself (Tugend, 1984a). The Youth Suicide Prevention Act of 1985, which would have provided funds to enable states, local governments, and private nonprofit agencies to implement prevention programs, was introduced in the U.S. House of Representatives (but has not yet become law). The U.S. Senate Subcommittee on Juvenile Justice held hearings on the topic of youth suicide, calling on authorities from NIMH to provide testimony (Blumenthal, 1985; Silver, 1985). The Centers for Disease Control (CDC) recognized youth suicide as a serious public health problem and began extensive research in this area (CDC, 1986; Tugend, 1984a).

The enormity of the problem prompted the legislatures of several states, including California, Florida, New Jersey, Louisiana, and Wisconsin, to mandate the establishment of suicide prevention programs in the schools. Lawmakers in Canadian provinces also pushed for support for programs aimed at suicide prevention. The California law provided for parent education, teacher training, and a curricular offering in the secondary school of 5 hours per year on the topic of suicide prevention. In Louisiana, a suicide prevention module was mandated in all secondary schools, generally in the 10th-grade health education course.

The most comprehensive state law related to the prevention of youth suicide to date was passed in 1984 by the Florida legislature. The Florida Youth Emotional Development and Suicide Prevention Act mandated the following:

1. Cooperation of the Departments of Health and Rehabilitative Services (HRS), Law Enforcement, and Education in the development of a statewide plan for the prevention of youth suicide.
2. The promulgation of district plans by local HRS task forces.
3. Training for all secondary teachers in the recognition of signs of severe emotional distress and appropriate interventions.
4. The inclusion of information on positive emotional development in the curriculum of the life management classes taught to 9th or 10th graders in the public schools.
5. The establishment of an interprogram task force to assist in implementing the state suicide prevention plan.
6. The development of training materials for use with adults and instructional materials for use with students.

Other rules, regulations, and policies were instituted as a result of the Florida law. The Department of Law Enforcement developed a handbook on youth suicide for law enforcement agents; the Florida State Department of Education added a requirement related to the prevention of youth suicide to its list of generic teacher certification competencies; and teacher training institutions within the state began to provide information about youth suicide to existing graduate and undergraduate courses.

Where there were no state or province guidelines, communities and school districts established their own programs aimed at the prevention of youth suicide. Among those districts are Bergen County, New Jersey; Dayton, Ohio; Denver, Colorado; Fairfax County, Virginia; Houston, Texas; Ithaca, New York; Minneapolis, Minnesota; Salt Lake City, Utah; and Vancouver, British Columbia. There are approximately 50 such programs across the United States (Perlman, cited in Viadero, 1987) as well as a number of others in Canada.

VARIATIONS IN SCHOOL PROGRAMS

Suicide prevention programs that have been established in the schools vary in terms of a number of variables, such as the setting in which the program is presented, time allotted to instruction, types of material presented, the credentials of the instructor, and the financial and human resources available. The settings have ranged from small groups in a counselor's office or a classroom to huge gatherings in the school auditorium. Materials have run the gamut from very positive information on enhancing self-esteem to potentially harmful screening instruments that give students the opportunity to select, among several options, the methods they might choose to kill themselves (without the option of "none of the above"). Some schools have established instructional units within existing courses that allow for discussion over a period of a full semester or even an entire school year; other schools have opted for single presentations by an "expert" with no follow-up. Some programs have been in effect for some time and are well accepted, while others have been established only recently and are viewed with concern. In some districts, suicide prevention information has been included in the school curriculum for more than 10 years, incorporated into health education or home economics classes—wherever topics such as "life skills," "personal growth," or "emotional health" are discussed. In other districts, school boards have refused to allow the classroom presentation of any material on suicide.

The reactions of the teachers and other personnel who work directly with the students also vary considerably. Some teachers and counselors are comfortable with the topic; others are afraid of parent disapproval, lawsuits, or the possibility of contagion. A psychologist who serves several public schools, including a high school, commented, "The faculty won't touch this stuff; they would rather wait for my visit. Some day that will be too late."

REASONS FOR CONCERN

According to Ross (1985), the educator's reluctance to offer information about suicide prevention directly to students may stem from (a) fears regarding the possibility of contagion, (b) fear that manipulative youngsters might use suicide threats as a means of control, (c) ambivalent feelings of compassion and anger toward suicidal youth, (d) denial that suicide is relevant to adolescents, and (e) concern that the school would be blamed for a student's suicidal behavior.

Although Ross suggested that such perceptions should not stand in the way of suicide prevention programs, these concerns are not unfounded. Schools have often been blamed for the deviant behavior (including suicidal actions) of students. Further, there are several recent cases in which parents of children who have killed themselves have brought legal action against the schools, claiming that the school authorities were in some way responsible for the deaths (Hildebrand, 1987; "School Districts," 1986). These court cases have not yet been resolved.

OTHER AWARENESS AND INTERVENTION ACTIVITY

In addition to prevention programs supported by states and provinces, communities, school districts, and national organizations, many other activities related to public awareness and intervention have taken place across the continent. Numerous task forces and committees have been formed, workshops and conferences have been held, and there has been a veritable proliferation of literature on the topic. Almost every newspaper in North America has published special articles about the problem of youth suicide as well as reports of young people who have killed themselves. Major television networks and local channels have joined the campaign, broadcasting motion pictures and documentaries depicting the suicides of young people and the tragic effects on families and friends.

What were the outcomes of this activity? The results of this tremendous increase in activity related to youth suicide have been equivocal. In some communities in which a suicide prevention program has been implemented, a decrease in the rate of suicide among young people has been reported (Tugend, 1984b). In other communities, however, there has been a marked increase in both completed suicides and attempts after the program was put into place. Parents, educators, and mental health professionals have expressed concern that the suicides and attempts may have been precipitated by the activities that were planned for the purpose of prevention.

"CATCH 22" IN SUICIDE PREVENTION

The quandary facing the schools is a "Catch 22" (Guetzloe, 1985a). Suicide prevention has been added to the domain of school responsibility, but very little information has been available regarding appropriate (or safe) instructional techniques and materials. Educators have looked to current research for direction, but the issue of whether school suicide prevention programs might trigger suicidal behavior is still unresolved, with professionals arguing on both sides of the question. Further, there are no empirical data that support the efficacy of school suicide prevention programs. There is, in fact, a paucity of data to support the effectiveness of any type of suicide prevention program.

Lack of Research on Program Outcomes

Almost 20 years ago, Shneidman called for "carefully planned programs in massive public education" (1970c, p. 148) as a means of securing lay cooperation in detecting and referring potential suicides. He also emphasized the importance of assessing the outcomes of such programs.

> The effects and effectiveness of such a program of public education should be observed through scientifically controlled studies . . . . The unanticipated effects of publicizing and popularizing the topic of suicide prevention would have to be constantly appraised during any mass education efforts. We do not know what either the short-term or the long-term effects of such a program might be. (Shneidman, 1970c, p. 149)

The public education campaign began without the scientific studies. The effects have not been evaluated.

Suicide—The Last Taboo

Massive public education programs have been implemented for purposes of combatting other major problems in the areas of public health and safety, such as Acquired Immune Deficiency Syndrome (AIDS), heart and lung disease, cancer, child abuse, crime, and fire. School programs have been established for purposes of addressing such topics as marriage and the family, drug and alcohol abuse, and sex education. Some of these subjects have been (and continue to be) extremely controversial; but it is suicide, because of its related stigma, that has been labeled "the last taboo" (Tugend, 1984b).

For many years, some suicidologists have argued that addressing the taboos related to suicide would reduce fear, encourage those in distress to seek help, and enhance the possibility of rescue by others (Ross, 1985; Shneidman, 1970b). Other researchers have warned, however, that those working in suicide prevention must be "exceedingly careful," and that taboos and stigma may be necessary barriers to limit suicidal behavior (Tugend, 1984a, p. 12).

POSITIVE AND NEGATIVE TRENDS

Most of the current trends related to youth suicide are encouraging, including (a) the establishment of school and district procedures related to detection and referral of depressed and suicidal students; (b) the provision of training for educators, parents, mental health professionals, and law enforcement agents; and (c) cooperation between school and nonschool professionals in planning and implementing intervention programs. Within the schools, suicide prevention programs often reflect cooperative efforts between regular and special education, collaboration with families and community agencies, and modifications in the school curriculum for purposes of meeting the needs of students in distress. Further, the numbers of crisis centers, hotlines, and other suicide prevention agencies continue to increase, and many communities have attempted to provide comprehensive health and social services for children at risk.

On the other hand, there are troubling trends, such as (a) competition and turfguarding among community agencies and national organizations ostensibly devoted to the cause of suicide prevention; (b) a rash of court cases, as mentioned previously, related to suicides and emotional problems in students; and (c) the ubiquitous threat of contagion.

In conclusion, the problem of youth suicide has become, within the past decade, a topic of considerable public interest and activity. The prevention of youth suicide has now been added to the ever-lengthening list of school concerns. Because of the considerable controversy related to this topic, educators should proceed with caution in developing plans for intervention within the school setting.

> Never before, in the history of mankind, have so many spent so much time, money, and energy—with so many means of communication—on the topic of suicide. There is no way to foretell the effects. Those who work with depressed and suicidal youth must hope for what the physician promises—Primum non nocere—"First of all, do not harm." (Guetzloe, 1987, p. 25)

4. Research: Problems, Trends, and Issues

The problems encountered in the study of suicide have been discussed by many researchers over the years. Maris (1981) has discussed some of these still-unresolved issues, including the following:

1. Completed suicide is still a rare occurrence, and there is probably never a single cause.
2. Although the retrospective research design appears to be the most practical procedure available, using significant others as informants introduces the possibility of error.
3. There are no standardized criteria for the classification of self-inflicted deaths.
4. Most researchers use either vital statistics or individual case histories as data sources, either of which, by itself, is inappropriate. Death certificates provide only information about the individual at the time of death, "a snapshot, when what is needed is something like a movie of the life and death styles of the suicidal individual" (p. 6). Individual case histories are not standardized, are based on clinical judgment, and are usually not representative samples of both completers and attempters.

The most obvious problem of all, according to Maris, is that in this area of research "the respondents cannot respond" (1981, p. 5). Information pertaining to completed suicides is generally obtained from survivors, whose judgments may be colored by grief, confusion, or feelings of guilt.

PROBLEMS IN STUDYING SUICIDE ATTEMPTERS

Similar problems are related to the reliability of data used in studies of suicide attempters. In studying suicide attempters who survived, Kubie found that memory of an attempt was often distorted by repression, guilt, and "almost dream-like elaborations" (1969, p. 83) that sometimes occurred when the attempters were toxic from medications or the loss of blood. Kubie suggested that, for these individuals, death had become "a kind of abstraction" (p. 83), and that their testimony was obviously unreliable.

PROBLEMS IN STUDYING YOUTH SUICIDE

The collection, analysis, and interpretation of data pertaining to suicidal behavior in young people is even more difficult. Berman (cited in Strother, 1986) has noted that most of the studies of suicidal children have been relatively unsophisticated and that they are usually of children who have attempted suicide, who may differ considerably from those who succeed in killing themselves. Significant research, according to Berman, should (a) focus on young people whose suicidal behavior is most lethal and (b) make use of control groups.

A psychiatrist from the NIMH suicide research unit has cited a number of flaws in studies of youth suicide, including those related to underreporting, untrained observers, and other methodological problems (Blumenthal, cited in Cuniberti, 1983). The results of many studies of youth suicide must therefore be viewed as inconclusive.

Analysis of Suicide Notes

Some research has been based on information derived from the analysis of suicide notes. Authorities have suggested that suicide notes offer an opportunity to gain insights into the thoughts and feelings of suicidal individuals, particularly since they were written in the context of suicidal behavior (Shneidman & Farberow, 1957, 1961). Many young people, however, do not leave suicide notes. Further, suicide notes by children and adolescents often contain statements specifically freeing survivors of responsibility which, according to Hendin, "are usually to be read psychologically as meaning the opposite" (1985, p. 31).

Psychological Autopsy

Most of the information regarding problems that may have contributed to a suicide is generally gathered from survivors in a procedure called a "psychological autopsy." This procedure was initiated by Dr. Theodore Curphey, Chief Medical Examiner-Coroner of Los Angeles, in cooperation with the Los Angeles Suicide Prevention Center in 1959 (Curphey, 1968; Shneidman & Mandelkorn, 1970).

In a psychological autopsy, death investigation teams attempt to discover whether the deceased, during the last days of life, actually intended to die. Clues are gleaned by carefully assessing information gathered from interviewing family members, friends, physicians, and others. If the investigators learn that the deceased had been depressed, had seen a physician recently, or had spoken or acted in such a way that indicated suicidal intent, the death can be classified as suicidal.

The investigations following the suicidal death of a young person usually involve the questioning of the immediate family, friends, teachers, and others who were close to the child in an attempt to shed some light on the cause of the tragedy. Such information may naturally be colored by the devastating effects of the suicide on the survivors. Further, the subtle clues of a youngster's suicidal intent may not have been evident before his or her death. In some cases, family survivors of youth suicide have said, during an interview closely following the child's death, that they could not remember whether they had really observed certain behaviors in the deceased or if they were remembering things that someone else had told them. Data gathered in this fashion may be neither valid nor reliable.

Psychological Autopsy in Cause of Death Investigations. In recent years, psychological autopsies—or "psychiatric autopsies," if the investigator is a psychiatrist—have been routinely used by medical examiners to determine the cause of death in hospital suicides or in cases where there is doubt as to cause (Scanlan, 1987). Insurance companies often use medical consultants as investigators to contest accidental death claims if there is reason to suspect that the death was a suicide.

Psychological Autopsy as Evidence in a Criminal Trial. In November 1987, for the first time, the findings of a psychological autopsy were entered as evidence in a criminal trial. Based on the study of a young girl's school and medical records and transcripts of depositions taken from her friends and relatives, a psychiatrist testified that the girl "was involved in an abusive relationship with her mother that was a substantial contributing cause to her suicide" (Jacobs, cited in Scanlan, 1987, p. 1D). The mother was convicted of causing her daughter to commit suicide. The technique is not without critics, however, both in and out of the courtroom. According to an expert in both psychiatry and law, "psychiatric testimony is inherently unreliable if the person being testified about cannot be or has not been examined" (Applebaum, cited in Scanlan, 1987, p. 2D).

CATEGORIES AND CLASSIFICATIONS OF SUICIDAL BEHAVIOR

Since the late 19th century, researchers have made numerous attempts to classify suicides for purposes of understanding this phenomenon and its causes. Suicides have been categorized according to such factors as age, social class, race, religion, geographical location, marital status, motivations, methods, purposes, prevailing conditions, precipitating events, the degree of intent to die, and whether or not the suicide was completed (Bender & Schilder, 1937; CDC, 1985, 1986; Gastil, 1971; Hendin, 1982; Marks & Abernathy, 1974; Menninger, 1933; Peck, 1985; Shaffer, 1974; Shneidman, 1966; Stengel, 1969; Toolan, 1962). For example, Bender and Schilder (1937) noted that suicidal children's motives included (a) the wish to punish parents, (b) the wish to escape from an unbearable situation, (c) the wish to achieve a pleasant state, and (d) the wish to be reunited with a dead relative.

Toolan (1962) also classified children and adolescents who attempted suicide into categories based on causes or motivations, including (a) anger internalized as depression or guilt, (b) an attempt to manipulate others to gain love or affection, (c) a signal of distress, (d) a reaction to feelings of disintegration, and (e) a desire to rejoin a dead relative.

According to an educator who is involved with suicide prevention in the schools, "the demographics, the profiles of students 'predisposed to suicide,' are of very little benefit in predicting suicidal behavior. Theories still abound, but answers don't" (Lieberman, cited in "Suicidal Students," Luty, 1985, p. 4).

The prediction of suicide would also raise a moral or ethical issue, in that, as discussed by Anderson (1981), the accurate prediction of suicide in itself constitutes a clinical failure. "Ethically, if we identify an individual at high risk, some intervention should be made on the individual's behalf" (Anderson, 1981, p. 53). Accurate prediction could also become a legal issue; if a child is identified as suicidal, then the family (or the school) may become responsible for preventing the child's suicide.

Peck (1985) has listed categories of youth suicide that may have implications for selecting appropriate interventions, including (a) the very young with learning disabilities, (b) the crisis suicide, (c) the loner, (d) the acting-out of depression, and (e) suicide as a form of communication. According to Peck, 75%-80% of youth suicides may fit into these categories. Although the categories were derived from studies of young people who completed suicide, Peck has suggested that they may also have implications for certain types of therapeutic interventions with youngsters who attempt or threaten suicide.

CURRENT MAJOR TRENDS IN RESEARCH

Within the past several years, there has been a considerable increase in the number of major research studies focused on youth suicide. Particular areas of interest have been the rising suicide rates, which were the focus of the CDC report on youth suicide surveillance (CDC, 1986); risk factors associated with suicidal behavior; the contagious nature of suicide (including the effects of the media); suicide clusters; the development of procedures for the assessment of suicidal intent; and the relationship of suicidal behavior to stress, depression, and other psychiatric disorders.

Research on Program Effectiveness

Although many suicide prevention programs have been implemented in school districts across the continent, there have been very few reports of outcomes. This problem, as mentioned previously, is not peculiar to school programs. For example, researchers have found that the number of mental health professionals (such as psychiatrists, social workers, and psychologists) in a certain community apparently does not affect the suicide rate (Glasser, Amdur, & Backstrand, 1985). Further, crisis hotlines have not been found to lower the suicide rate among young people in a particular community (Garfinkel, cited in Strother, 1986). Crisis intervention centers, however, may reduce the suicide rates among certain types of suicidal individuals.

Miller, Coombs, Leeper, and Barton (1984) compared the suicide rates of counties in the United States in which crisis intervention centers were established with the rates of counties in which there were no such agencies. Although there was little overall change in rates for all counties over a 5-year period, the counties in which there were crisis centers experienced a decrease in rates of one specific group—young White females (ages 24 or younger). The authors estimated that crisis centers, if available in all communities, might save the lives of 600 young females per year.

Evaluations of School Suicide Prevention Programs

Ross (1985) collected data on the following in an assessment of a districtwide high school prevention program:

1. Changes in the numbers of potentially suicidal students identified by school personnel.
2. Changes in the numbers of adolescents calling the suicide and crisis center.
3. Frequency and types of requests by school personnel for consultation with trainers.
4. Evaluations by participants.
5. Observable community response.

Increases were reported in the numbers of students identified by school personnel, the numbers of adolescents calling the crisis center, and the frequency of requests by school personnel for consultation. The types of requests for help by school personnel changed over time from asking what kind of action to take to requests for validation of action already taken. The responses of both school personnel and community leaders were favorable, and requests for the training programs were received from other high school districts. Ross (1985) concluded that school programs for suicide prevention are feasible and that these programs can receive enthusiastic support from students, school personnel, and the community.

The Teen Stress and Suicide Prevention (TSSP) project in the state of Ohio recently completed its annual program evaluation ("Teen Stress," 1988). A total of 6,611 students in grades 6 through 12, representing 55 schools and youth groups from 9 counties, participated in the TSSP project from August 1986 to August 1987. Students' reactions and test results included the following: 76% reported that they had learned something from the program; 81% reported that the program helped them to learn about causes, signs, and ways to deal with stress; 75% found the program helpful in learning the warning signs of possible suicide; 16% reported that they would like more information on stress management and suicide prevention; and 89% correctly answered questions on stress management techniques and suicide myths.

Older students (in grades 10 through 12) more often than younger ones (in grades 6 through 9) reported that the program information was not totally new to them. The older students, however, reported at the same rate (slightly higher than 80%) as did the younger ones that the information was helpful.

Researchers at Columbia University, at the request of the Governor of New Jersey, are currently investigating the results of school-based suicide prevention programs in that state. The results of that research are not yet available.

DIRECTIONS FOR FUTURE RESEARCH

Hawton (1986) has suggested several directions for future research on youth suicide, including (a) comparing the coping responses of adolescent suicide attempters with those of other adolescents, (b) investigating the effectiveness of different forms of aftercare following suicide attempts, and (c) studying the short-term and long-term outcomes of suicide attempts. He has further suggested more adequate evaluation of intensive treatment programs based on behavioral approaches. According to Hawton, such programs have produced encouraging results with suicidal adults.

What helps young people to survive? If a community or school district reports a reduction in the incidence of suicide or other suicidal behavior, there is no way to know what made the difference—a school program, the increased vigilance of parents, the efforts of counselors or friends, maturation, or an increase in self-satisfaction on the part of some young person who might otherwise have added to the statistics. Rather than focusing primarily on those students who succeeded in ending their lives, perhaps researchers should investigate the reasons formerly suicidal youngsters have decided to live. Knowing what made life more attractive—and death less attractive—for these young people might lead to new directions in intervention.

5. Current Extent of the Problem—Facts and Statistics

According to reports of mortality statistics in the United States (NCHS, 1987), suicide is the second leading cause of death among persons ages 15 to 24 years and the sixth leading cause of death among youngsters ages 5 to 14 years. Suicide has also been recognized as the second leading cause of death among college students (American Psychiatric Association, 1985; Silver, 1985). Suicide is also the most common psychiatric emergency ("Suicide, Part 1," 1986), as well as one of the four major problems—along with sexual issues, substance abuse, and antisocial behavior—to be encountered by mental health professionals who work with adolescents (Shrier & Johnson, 1985). Further, although there is a paucity of official data regarding this population, suicidal behavior is also a problem among very young children (Pfeffer, 1986; Rosenthal & Rosenthal, 1984).

It should be noted, however, that suicide is not only a problem among the young; suicide is also the eighth leading cause of death for all Americans (NCHS, 1987). There are also indications that the suicide rate continues to increase with age, reaching its peak in the elderly (Rutter, 1986). Regardless of country of birth, the suicide rate for males increases linearly with age (Dublin, 1963; Maris, 1969, 1981; Rutter, 1986). In comparison with other countries that have long been recognized as suicide prone—such as Japan and Sweden—the United States once had a low rate of suicide among young people (Hendin, 1982). The suicide rate for young males in the United States is now among the highest in the world (Hendin, 1985).

According to Statistics Canada, a governmental statistics agency, the rate of suicide among young Canadians rose alarmingly between 1961 and 1981 ("Youth Suicide," 1985). Suicide is now the second leading cause of death among young people in Canada, ranking below only traffic accidents.

The problem of suicidal behavior among children and youth is not restricted to the North American continent. Unusual increases in the rates of youth suicide have been reported in other countries, including Australia, Austria, Denmark, England, Finland, Israel, Japan, and Sweden (Cantor, cited in Zeitlin, 1985; Farberow, 1985). The increases in rate, however, are particularly pronounced in the United States, Canada, and countries with similar life styles (Farberow, 1985).

MISREPORTING OR UNDERREPORTING OF SUICIDE

Researchers generally agree that the official statistics on suicide are inaccurate and that suicide—particularly among the young—may be misreported or underreported (Barraclough, 1973; Centers for Disease Control, 1985, 1986; Connell, 1972; Maris, 1981; McClure, 1984: Miller, 1975; Peck, 1985; Pfeffer, 1986; Shaffer & Fisher, 1981; Silver, 1985; Wilkins, 1970). Some authorities have even questioned the use of statistical methods in studying suicide because of the problems involved in obtaining reliable information (Baechler, 1979; Douglas, 1967; Hawton, 1986; Maris, 1981). In a recent survey of medical examiners, more than half the respondents felt that the reported number of suicides is probably less than half of the actual number (Jobes, Berman, & Josselsen, 1986).

Wilkins (1970) studied the reporting of suicide in a sample of 1,311 individuals of all ages who had previously contacted a suicide prevention center. Nineteen months after the last person had contacted the center, 17 of these individuals had died, and only 4 of the deaths had been certified as suicides. After an intensive review of each case, Wilkins concluded that the true suicide rate among the group was probably two or three times higher than the recorded rate.

WHY ARE THE REPORTS INACCURATE?

The limited accuracy and reliability of suicide statistics are, in part, attributable to the lack of a commonly accepted definition of suicide (CDC, 1986). Judgments by physicians, coroners, and medical examiners play a part in the process by which suicides are classified, but there are no uniform criteria for the classification of suicide to guide these judgments. Coroners or medical examiners in neighboring communities may use very different criteria to classify deaths as suicide. For example, one coroner may refuse to classify any death as a suicide unless there is a signed suicide note from the victim, while another coroner may classify a death as a suicide without any note, based on autopsy evidence and interviews with the family of the victim.

The Violence Epidemiology Branch of the Center for Health Promotion and Education has acknowledged the difficulty in obtaining accurate statistics, citing several reasons for inaccuracies: (a) inadequate information, (b) certifier bias or error, and (c) the lack of a death certificate (CDC, 1985).

Inadequate Information

If there is no explicit communication from the victim (such as a suicide note or previous verbal comments) that the death was self-inflicted, the death may be certified as "undetermined" (CDC, 1985, p. 5). There is also the possibility that family or other survivors may consciously or unconsciously withhold information that is necessary for determination of suicide.

Certifier Bias or Error

In deference to, or because of pressure from, the family or other survivors, the certifier may rule that the death was accidental. The stigma attached to suicide causes many problems for survivors. Further, insurance policies may not cover hospital, ambulance, or other expenses resulting from completed or attempted suicide, and death benefits from insurance may be reduced. Pressure may also be brought to bear by those who wish to preserve the reputation of the neighborhood or community. It is also possible that the certifier may rule in error. Basing judgments on the same information, two certifiers may rule differently as to cause of death.

Lack of a Death Certificate

Some suicide deaths may not be recorded because the bodies are never found. This situation is likely to occur in cases of deaths by certain methods (e.g., drowning or jumping from a high bridge).

MISREPORTING OR UNDERREPORTING OF YOUTH SUICIDE

Suicide among young people may be misreported or underreported to an even greater extent than suicide among adults. Shaffer (1974) reviewed coroners' records for a group of children whose deaths were designated as of undetermined cause and concluded that most of those deaths were probably suicides.

The stigma attached to suicide is particularly devastating for survivors when the victim is a child. A chief medical examiner in a large midwestern county reported that he never certified a child's death as suicide (regardless of the child's age and even if a suicide note was left) because he did not wish to stigmatize the parents (Anthony, 1975). There is also the possibility that death by a child's own hand may be accidental.

Hawton (1986), who has studied this problem from an international perspective, has summarized the reasons for the underreporting of suicide specifically among young people as follows:

1. The relative rarity of suicide in young people may make those responsible for determining the cause of death unlikely to consider suicide as an explanation.
2. The widely held belief that children rarely commit suicide may create a tendency to report deaths of young people as accidental.
3. Those responsible for reporting suicide may be consciously or unconsciously attempting to protect the family from the extra burden that a certification of suicide might cause.
4. The predominant religious beliefs of a particular culture or locality might have a bearing on the verdict of suicide.

DEVELOPMENT OF OPERATIONAL CRITERIA FOR REPORTING SUICIDE

Representatives from several national organizations have been working to develop operational criteria that should make the classification of suicide more accurate and reliable throughout the United States. Organizations involved in this effort include the American Academy of Forensic Sciences, American Association of Suicidology, Association of Vital Records and Health Statistics, Centers for Disease Control (CDC), International Association of Coroners and Medical Examiners, National Association of Counties, National Association of Medical Examiners, and the National Center for Health Statistics (NCHS) (CDC, 1986).

REDUCING THE RATES: A NATIONAL HEALTH OBJECTIVE

Because of the dramatic increase in the rates of suicide among American youth, the U.S. Department of Health and Human Services (DHHS) established a specific objective—that by 1990, the rate of suicide among young people 15–24 years of age should be below 11 per 100,000 population (CDC, 1986; Public Health Service, 1980). (The decision was made in response to the reported rate of 12.4 in 1978, which was later revised to 12.1 with updated information from the 1980 census.) Monitoring and promoting progress toward this objective became the responsibility of CDC and the National Institute of Mental Health (NIMH). To fulfill this responsibility, it was necessary to document the rates of suicide in this age group. No detailed compilation of national suicide statistics had been published since 1964 (CDC, 1986).

Youth Suicide Surveillance by CDC

In November 1986, CDC issued a surveillance report on suicide deaths among young Americans ages 15 to 24. The report contains an analysis of vital statistics based on death certificates and provides recent and accurate information on trends in youth suicide from a national perspective. The following are some of the findings reported in the CDC document:

1. Over the past three decades, the suicide rate among young people in the United States has increased dramatically. Over the 30-year period, the rate increased from 4.5 to 12.3 deaths per 100,000 in the population ages 15 to 24.
2. Between 1970 and 1980, the suicide rate among American youth ages 15 to 24 increased from 8.8 to 12.3 deaths per 100,000. During that period, the rate for the remainder of the population remained stable.
3. The year that ranked highest in the rate of youth suicide was 1977. The rate for that year was 13.3 per 100,000.
4. The increase in the rate of suicide among young people is due primarily to an increase in the rate among young males. The rate for males increased by 50% (from 13.5 to 20.2 per 100,000 population). By 1980, the ratio of suicides committed by males to those committed by females was almost 5 to 1 in this age group.
5. Most of the young male victims were White (89%). Suicide rates for young males of Black and other races also increased (20.2%) but remained lower than those of young White males.
6. The rate for all young females increased by 2% during the period from 1970 to 1980. The rate for young White females increased by 9.5%, but the rate for females of Black and other races decreased by 34.1% and were lower in 1980 than in 1970.
7. The suicide rates for young people ages 20 to 24 (16.1 per 100,000) during the period from 1970 to 1980 were consistently higher than

the rates for those ages 15 to 19 (8.5 per 100,000). During this period, however, the rate of increase was greater for the younger group.

8. The most frequent method of suicide for males ages 15 to 24 years of age was firearms and explosives (primarily firearms). The second most common method for males was hanging, strangulation, or suffocation. The primary change over the period from 1970 to 1980 was an increase in the use of firearms and a decrease in poisoning.

9. There was a marked increase in firearm suicides among young females accompanied by a decrease in suicide by poisoning (primarily by drugs).

Limitations of the CDC Study

Despite the comprehensive nature of the statistical information included in the CDC report, there are certain limitations, which have been cited by CDC (1986), related to the use of vital statistics information in planning for suicide prevention activity. The information available from NCHS is drawn from death certificates, which contain very little information that would be helpful in determining the actual causes of suicide. The variables available for analysis are age, race, sex, place of residence, place of occurrence of death, date of death, and cause of death. There is no information regarding the victim's personal or family history of suicide, mental illness, or substance abuse; family structure; socioeconomic status; or recent life changes.

There is also a time lag of 2 to 3 years resulting from the current system for collecting vital statistics data from cities, counties, and states and subsequently compiling them in a national center (CDC, 1986). This system does not support timely monitoring of trends or the swift detection of increases in rates in discrete or localized areas. States or communities that provide for analysis of suicide rates within their own jurisdictions may be able to detect increases in rates more quickly and initiate intervention in a more timely fashion.

Unofficial Statistical Information

In addition to the data reported by CDC, Statistics Canada, and other governmental agencies, statistical information regarding suicidal behavior in children and adolescents can be derived from the numerous studies that have been conducted on this topic. Several researchers have reported information of particular interest to educators.

Race, Social Status, and Ethnicity. Pfeffer and associates (Pfeffer & Plutchik, 1982; Pfeffer, Plutchik, Mizruchi, & Lipkins,1985) studied consecutive admissions to both municipal hospital psychiatric inpatient and outpatient units and similar units in a voluntary hospital setting. They found similar prevalence figures for suicidal behavior in children from different social status backgrounds and racial or ethnic groups. These researchers concluded that race, ethnicity, and social status are not major factors in determining the prevalence of suicidal behavior in children (Pfeffer, 1986).

Suicidal Behavior in Young Children. Suicidal behavior has been noted in very young children (Pfeffer, 1986; Rosenthal & Rosenthal, 1984). There is, however, a paucity of official data regarding rates of suicide among the very young.

Suicides of very young children may often be either undetected or unreported. Further, the self-inflicted deaths of children under the age of 10 are generally classified by NCHS as accidents unless there is conclusive evidence to the contrary. The rationale for this classification is the prevailing belief that young children do not understand the finality of death. Children must be old enough to realize the consequences of their actions before suicide is officially determined.

Suicidal Behavior in Preschool Children. Rosenthal and Rosenthal (1984) examined 16 preschoolers, ranging in age from 2 1/2 to 5 years, who were referred to a university child psychiatry outpatient clinic after seriously injuring themselves or attempting to do so. Thirteen of these children had made multiple suicide attempts, using methods that included setting themselves on fire, ingesting prescription drugs, jumping from high places, running into fast traffic, jumping into water, head-banging, and throwing themselves down stairs.

Some of the children perceived death as reversible, but others were aware of the finality of death. They wanted to die to obtain reunion with loved ones, a chance to be cared for after death, or escape from an unbearable life situation. Thirteen of the children were unwanted by their parents and had been physically abused.

When compared with matched controls who were behaviorally disordered but not suicidal, the suicidal children had significantly higher rates of running away, aggression directed at self, and depressive symptoms. Of the suicidal group, three-fourths showed neither pain nor crying after either suicide attempts or bona fide accidents.

Rosenthal and Rosenthal (1984) have suggested that primary caregivers should ask injured preschoolers about the circumstances of their "accidents" (p. 524) in cases of repeated episodes of injury, a high degree of family stress, physical abuse or neglect, actual or threatened severing of a relationship with a key nurturing figure, or aggressive behavior by the child. According to these authors, preschool children will readily admit suicidal intent if it is present. "The lethal potential of these suicidal behaviors and the ease with which they can be misconstrued as accidental in this age group suggest that we actively look for fire amid so much smoke" (p. 524).

Continuum of Suicidal Behavior

A number of researchers have found that there is a continuum of suicidal behavior in young people that includes suicidal ideas, threats, attempts, and completed suicide (Paykel, Myers, Lindenthal, & Tanner, 1974; Pfeffer, Conte, Plutchik, & Jerrett, 1979, 1980; Pfeffer, Solomon, Plutchik, Mizruchi, & Weiner, 1982; Pfeffer, Zuckerman, Plutchik, & Mizruchi, 1984). According to Giffin and Fesenthal (1982), approximately 80% of adolescents who commit suicide have made open threats beforehand. Other researchers have reported very little difference between adolescents who threatened suicide and those who completed the act (Marks & Haller, 1977). Such findings have been cited as a rationale for studying nonfatal suicidal behavior to understand completed suicide (Pfeffer, 1986). Further, suicide threats, gestures, and ideation are all generally considered to be warning signs of potential suicide. Maris (1981) has suggested that other types of self-destructive behavior in the young, including accident proneness or head-banging, may also be related to suicide.

Estimates of Suicide Attempts By Children and Adolescents. For every successful suicide by a young person there may be as many as 50 to 150 attempts (Klagsbrun, 1976; McIntyre, Angle, & Schlicht, 1977; Mishara, 1979). Recent estimates of the number of attempts per year among American adolescents range from 250,000 (Giovacchini, 1981) to 500,000 (Berman, 1986). These estimates, which are based on the number of reported suicides, do not take into account the probability that the actual number of suicides may be two or three times higher than the official statistics indicate (American Psychiatric Association, 1985).

Suicide attempts lead to the hospitalization of an estimated 12,000 youngsters ages 14 and under in the United States each year (Berman, 1986; Matter & Matter, 1984). According to Berman (1986), many attempts (as many as seven out of every eight) do not require medical treatment and are therefore not included in this estimate. Hospital personnel have noted that previous unreported attempts often become known when a more serious attempt requires medical attention. Further, the great majority of completed suicides are by individuals who have made previous attempts.

Suicidal Behaviors Among Normal Children and Youth. Suicidal thoughts, threats, gestures, and attempts have also been observed in normal children and adolescents. Pfeffer, Suckerman, Plutchik, and Mizruchi (1984) studied the prevalence of suicidal behavior in children with no history of psychiatric problems. A random sample of 101 children, ages 6 to 12, was selected from the school roster of 1,565 normal preadolescents in a metropolitan community of over 100,000 people. All children attending special education classes for either the emotionally disturbed or the neurologically impaired were excluded from the study. Although the subjects had no history of psychiatric disorder, approximately 12% had suicidal tendencies. All of the children and at least one parent of each (usually the mother) were interviewed by either a child psychiatrist or a child psychologist, who used a semi-structured approach. The children were asked specific questions about suicide such as "Have you ever thought of hurting yourself? Did you ever think of committing suicide? Did you ever try to commit suicide?" (p. 79). The suicidal ideas or actions reported by the children were similar to those expressed by young psychiatric patients in previous studies (Cohen-Sandler, Berman, & King, 1982; Pfeffer, Conte, et al., 1979, 1980; Pfeffer, Solomon, et al., 1982). Parental depression and suicidal behavior, especially among the mothers, were common in the group, and half the children showed signs of depression. According to Pfeffer (1985), these findings support the need for early recognition of suicidal tendencies because, until the children were interviewed for the study, they were not known to be having problems.

Ross (cited in Davis, 1985) surveyed a normal population of high school students and found that 12% of the seniors had made one or more previous suicide attempts. Heckel (cited in Davis, 1985) found that over 50% of the freshman class in a small urban college had contemplated suicide at least once. Based on these surveys, Davis (1985) predicted that, in a high school population of 2,000 students, there would be suicidal thoughts in as many as 20%–30%, suicide attempts by as many as 50 students each year, and one completed suicide every 4 years.

More recently, the CDC Division of Adolescent and School Health conducted a survey of 11,000 8th and 10th grade students in 20 states on such subjects as alcohol, sex, violence, and suicide. Of the respondents, 34% (25% of the boys and 42% of the girls) had thought seriously of ending their lives, and 15% had made serious attempts (Survey, 1989).

Youth Suicide Still a Rare Occurrence. Despite the current frightening statistics, youth suicide is still a relatively rare occurrence. Accidents claim by far the greatest number of victims among young people of all ages. In 1980, NCHS reported 8,537 accidents (the leading cause of death) and 142 suicides (the 10th major cause of death) in the 1- to 14-year age group (CDC, 1985). Among young people 15 to 24 years of age, there were 26,206 accidents; 6,647 homicides; and 5,239 suicides (CDC, 1985).

PREDICTIONS REGARDING FUTURE RATES OF YOUTH SUICIDE

Researchers have not reached agreement regarding predictions of future suicide rates among young people. Basing his conclusions on a trend analysis derived from data over the previous decade, Frederick (1985) predicted that, unless a significant intervention program is developed nationwide, the suicide rate among the young will continue to rise markedly into the next century. He has further predicted especially dramatic increases of 144% for males ages 10 through 14 and 146% for males ages 20 through 24. According to another researcher, however (Wetzel, cited in "Researcher," 1986), the suicide rate among teenagers is starting to decline and should decrease gradually over the next 5 years. A prediction from the American Psychiatric Association (1985) is that the rate will continue to be approximately 12 per 100,000 among people ages 15 to 24, which will account for approximately 5,000 deaths per year in the United States.

6. Are Exceptional Students at Risk for Suicide?

There is little accurate information regarding the rates of suicide among exceptional students, but several authors have suggested that the handicapped and gifted are at risk for suicidal behavior. Further, studies of children and youth who have committed suicide have revealed disproportionate numbers of exceptional children among the victims, although the youngsters may not have been so labeled by school authorities (Jan-Tausch, 1964; Peck, 1985; Shaffer, 1974). Suicidal behavior has been noted in children who are mentally retarded as well as in children of superior intelligence (Pfeffer, 1981). Exceptional children (including the gifted) may often suffer from feelings of helplessness, hopelessness, and low self-esteem, which may increase their vulnerability to suicidal behavior (Peck, 1985; Pfeffer, 1986). Further, handicapped children have been found to be disproportionately susceptible to abuse, which in turn may trigger suicidal thoughts and actions ("Child Abuse," 1987).

In an unpublished survey, Bryan and Herjanic (cited in Bryan & Herjanic, 1980) asked directors of programs for the handicapped whether there were cases of suicide, suicide attempts, or depression under treatment among the young people served by their facilities within the previous 10 years. Reports of suicide, attempts, and depression under treatment were received from programs serving the mentally retarded, the deaf, the orthopedically handicapped, individuals with cerebral palsy, and those with multiple sclerosis. Several respondents expressed concern that depression among the developmentally disabled might be overlooked or misdiagnosed.

SUICIDAL BEHAVIOR IN CHILDREN WITH SEVERE BEHAVIORAL DISORDERS

A severe behavior disorder is by far the most significant handicapping condition associated with suicidal behavior. Authorities from the National Institute of Mental Health (NIMH) (Blumenthal, 1985) have estimated that 60% of American teenagers who kill themselves are suffering from a mental disorder. These youngsters often fail to seek professional help, however, because they do not want to be thought of as mentally ill. Further, for a variety of reasons, they may not be referred within the school for special education assessment or placement. Knoblock (1983) described children who are depressed or suicidal as "children between the cracks," whose pain and needs are great but who are often unrecognized and unserved.

Many of the studies of completed suicide among children and adolescents have reported a high prevalence of psychiatric disorders, although suicidal tendencies may not have been previously noted. Shaffer (1974) studied all suicides recorded for children ages 14 and under during a 4-year period in England and Wales. Nine of the 30 youngsters had been either under the care of a psychiatrist or on a waiting list for a psychiatric appointment, but only two had been referred because of a previous suicide attempt. Six of the other victims had been recognized by school authorities as having emotional or conduct problems and were clients of welfare or probation agencies. Of the total number, 22 had exhibited antisocial behavior (including stealing, bullying, or truancy); 21 had shown signs of emotional problems such as depression or extreme fearfulness; and 17 children had exhibited both antisocial behavior and emotional problems.

Golumbek and Garfinkel (1983) reported that psychiatric disorders (primarily depressive) were evident in 25% of a group of 10- to 24-year-olds who killed themselves in Ontario, Canada. Cosand, Bourque, and Kraus (1982) studied two groups of young people who had committed suicide (15- to 19-year-olds and 20- to 24-year olds) and found that one-third of the younger group and one-half of the older group had previously shown signs of emotional instability, with depression the most common diagnosis. Among the younger subjects, 17% had received psychiatric treatment, as had slightly more of the older group. Suicidal behavior has also been noted in young people who have been diagnosed as childhood schizophrenics (Cosand et al., 1982; Golumbek & Garfinkel, 1983; Winn & Halla, 1966).

SUICIDAL BEHAVIOR AMONG PSYCHIATRIC HOSPITAL PATIENTS

Suicidal behavior is particularly prevalent among young psychiatric patients. Cohen-Sandler, Berman, and King (1982) found that 26% of 76 children consecutively admitted to a psychiatric inpatient unit had threatened or attempted suicide. In another sample of 58 children consecutively admitted to a municipal psychiatric hospital, 72% had suicidal ideas or had threatened or attempted suicide (Pfeffer, Conte, et al., 1979). Among all of the children referred for admission as inpatients, 33% exhibited suicidal tendencies, as did 33% of children treated in the outpatient clinic of the same hospital (Pfeffer, Conte, et al., 1979, 1980).

SUICIDAL BEHAVIOR IN CHILDREN WITH LEARNING DISABILITIES

Several researchers have noted that children and adolescents with learning disabilities are at risk for suicidal behavior. In a pilot study of all children under the age of 15 who had committed suicide in Los Angeles during a 3-year period (a total of 14 children), it was found that seven (50%) had been diagnosed as having learning disabilities (Peck, 1985). Researchers have also reported relationships between suicidal behavior and diminished problem-solving abilities (Levenson & Neuringer, 1971) and between cognitive deficits and depression, which is in turn related to suicidal behavior (Brumback, Staton, & Wilson, 1980).

According to Pfeffer (1981), the most important factor relating school problems to suicidal behavior appears to be the degree of the child's concern about poor achievement rather than the actual academic performance. Comparisons with peers and fears of punishment or scorn by parents contribute to feelings of low self-esteem, which may lead to suicidal thoughts and actions.

Suicidal Behavior and Visual-Motor Problems

Psychological testing of adolescents who had attempted suicide revealed a significant incidence of visual-motor problems suggestive of neurological dysfunction or learning disabilities among the population (Rohn, Sarles, Kenny, Reynolds, & Heald, 1977). In a study that compared the test scores of adolescent suicide attempters with those of a nonsuicidal control group, the attempters showed significantly more problems with visual-motor coordination than did the controls (Kenny, Rohn, Sarles, Reynolds, & Heald, 1979). At the time of the attempt, many of these learning problems had not been diagnosed. The school histories of the attempters also showed significantly more school problems (suspension, truancy, and behavior problems) and a higher rate of school failure than those of the controls.

Suicidal Behavior and Hyperactivity

A follow-up study of children who had been identified as hyperactive, including children with learning disabilities and neurologic dysfunction, found that these children continued to function poorly in academic areas during their teenage years and that they exhibited signs of social maladjustment. The children were described as having poor self-images and feelings of hopelessness, which are risk factors commonly associated with suicidal behavior (Weiss, et al., 1971).

SUICIDAL BEHAVIOR AND PHYSICAL DISORDERS

Among adults who commit suicide, poor health is an important contributing factor, particularly among the elderly (Fawcett & Susman, 1975; Hawton, 1986; Shneidman & Farberow, 1961), but physical illness has not often been cited as a factor in the completed suicides of children and adolescents (Hawton, 1986). Sathyavathi (1975), who found that 29% of her sample of suicides in India had been ill with such complaints as asthma or tonsillitis, suggested that the illness itself may not have been a factor in the suicides, but that illness may contribute to a child's being more vulnerable to distress caused by other factors, such as school failure or punishment by parents. Litman and Diller (1985), however, compared the histories of young suicide victims with those of living peers and found a trend toward more learning disability and more medical illness (including asthma) among the victims.

A disfiguring or debilitating injury is an important risk factor associated with depression and suicidal behavior among young people. Orthopedic patients, as stated in the section on statistics, have one of the highest rates of depression among children and youth (Kashani, Venske, & Millar, 1981). Fawcett and Susman (1975) noted a high prevalence of suicidal behavior among individuals with facial or body disfigurement.

In a sample of 50 adolescents, ages 13 to 18, who had taken drug overdoses, evidence of poor physical health was common (Hawton, O'Grady, Osborn, & Cole, 1982). MacGregor (1977) found a high incidence of suicide and attempted suicide among diabetic children. Suicidal behavior has also been reported in children with serious kidney problems (Abram, Moore, & Westerfelt, 1971; Bernstein, 1971; Khan, Herndon, & Ahmadian, 1971). According to Pfeffer (1986), children with severe psychopathology or serious life-threatening illness are at great risk for suicidal behavior. Many checklists used in the assessment of suicide risk include questions regarding the presence of injury or illness.

Recent evidence indicates that individuals who have been diagnosed as having AIDS are at high risk for suicide (Dodds, cited in "AIDS," 1987). The director of the Health Crisis Network of Miami, Florida, reported at a U.S. Senate Subcommittee hearing that 7 of 35 people who had tested positive for the human immunodeficiency virus (HIV) during the previous 2 1/2 months had committed suicide before their first counseling session. The agency had responded to the suicides by adopting a new policy that treats individuals with positive AIDS test results as high suicide risks.

Although no ages were reported for the victims, this problem is of particular importance for special education personnel. The numbers of children born with AIDS or indications of exposure to AIDS have shown a considerable recent increase, and many of these youngsters will be served by special education.

DEPRESSION AND SUICIDAL BEHAVIOR AMONG CHILDREN WITH HEARING IMPAIRMENTS

An administrator in a large school district noted high rates of depression, self-destructive behavior, and suicidal tendencies among children who had been diagnosed as either deaf or hearing impaired (Stovall, 1986, personal communication). She suggested that these students may suffer from isolation, difficulties in understanding and expressing their feelings, and unreasonably high expectations.

SUICIDAL BEHAVIOR IN YOUTH WITH MENTAL RETARDATION

There are very few references to suicide in the literature on mental retardation, but suicidal behavior has been noted, as mentioned previously, in populations of mentally retarded youth (Pfeffer, 1981).

There are occasional news reports of suicides by mentally retarded youth. The following account specifically mentioned that the young victim was mentally retarded.

An 18-year-old hanged himself in a county jail. He had been kept separate from the rest of the jail population because he was mentally retarded.

He was found hanging from the shower rod. He had wrapped the shower curtain around his neck and let his body go limp.

He was in jail waiting to be taken to the psychiatric unit in another jail. He had been charged with child molesting and one count of threatening and intimidation.

SUICIDAL BEHAVIOR IN THE GIFTED AND TALENTED

The director for gifted and talented on the National Education Association's Caucus for Educators of Exceptional Children has suggested that the suicide rate among gifted students is "among the highest" (Innis, cited in "Educating the Gifted," 1987, p. 5). Other authors have also expressed concern regarding the susceptibility of gifted youngsters to emotional problems that could lead to suicidal behavior (Delisle, 1982, 1986; Lajoie, 1981; Leroux, 1986; McCants, 1985; Willings & Arsenault, 1986).

A nationwide survey by Who's Who Among American High School Students revealed that 30% of the nation's top high school juniors and seniors have considered suicide (Hidlay, 1988). The survey, which was released in September 1988, polled 2,024 high-achieving students from public, private, and parochial schools who are listed in the directory. The students had grade averages of A or B and usually also excelled in other activities, such as school organizations, sports, or community service. Nearly half of the respondents knew someone who had either committed or attempted suicide. The major reasons listed by the students for suicidal thoughts or actions were (a) a feeling of worthlessness, (b) a feeling of isolation and loneliness, (c) pressure to achieve, and (d) a fear of failure.

SUICIDAL BEHAVIOR AMONG DELINQUENT AND INCARCERATED YOUTH

The inclusion of a discussion of delinquent and incarcerated in this chapter is by no means intended to imply that all such young people have been identified as either handicapped or gifted. There is compelling evidence, however, that handicapped youth are over-represented in the population of youthful offenders (Brown & Courtless, 1982; Coffey, 1983; Eggleston, 1984; Morgan, 1979; Rutherford, Nelson, & Wofford, 1985; Santamour & West, 1979; Zeleny, 1983).

Studies by Maris (1969), Breed (1970), and Connell (1965) all found that suicidal ideation was particularly prevalent among young people who had recently been arrested. Shaffer (1974) found a high rate of delinquency among children in England and Wales who had committed suicide.

Suicide has been a serious problem among young inmates of jails and police lockups in the United States. A study by a medical examiner's office of the deaths in local jails and holding facilities revealed that 20 of the 25 deaths reported over a 2-year period were suicides (Charle, 1981). This problem was most acute among children and adolescents who are housed in adult facilities (Charle, 1981). There were also marked indications of escalation during 1988.

7. Risk Factors Associated with Suicidal Behavior

Despite many investigations by researchers from many disciplines, the exact causes of suicide are still a mystery. Authorities are in agreement, however, that the reasons are complex, that there is no single cause, and that the factors associated with suicide in children and adolescents often differ from those in adults. Many problems that contribute to feelings of stress, depression, helplessness, hopelessness, and low self-esteem may in turn lead to suicidal behavior in children and youth.

Rather than attempting to explain the precise causes of suicide, which are known only to the victim, authorities prefer to discuss risk factors and precipitating events. These problems may be divided roughly according to duration, with a risk factor being of a long-term nature (in place for some time before the suicide) and a precipitating event being rather a crisis that immediately precedes a suicidal action—the proverbial "straw that breaks a camel's back." Some of the risk factors commonly cited in the literature are briefly discussed here. Where possible, they are loosely categorized in terms of possible origin, such as (a) biological factors, (b) psychiatric disorders, (c) family problems, (d) environmental and sociocultural factors, and (e) factors related to learning and cognition.

It is important to understand that the presence of any one (or more) of these risk factors does not mean that a certain child will be suicidal; neither does the absence of these problems ensure that a child will not commit suicide. They are simply situations and problems that have been noted by mental health professionals and researchers as among the most important factors related to suicidal behavior in children and adolescents.

PREVIOUS SUICIDAL BEHAVIOR

Authorities are in agreement that a previous suicide attempt is a critical indicator of risk for suicidal behavior. Further, recurring attempts may become more dangerous. Whether or not the cry for help goes unheeded, the lethality of method (and therefore the risk) may increase, and unintended death may occur. Further, thoughts or threats may escalate to attempts.

Shaffi, Carrigan, Whittinghill, and Derrick (1985) interviewed families, friends, and close acquaintances of 20 young people between the ages of 12 and 19 who had recently committed suicide. The researchers found that the victims had exhibited a number of warning signs, including suicide attempts, threats, or ideas; alcohol or drug abuse; and histories of antisocial behavior.

BIOLOGICAL FACTORS RELATED TO SUICIDE

In the field of medicine, research has focused on biological factors that may be related to suicidal behavior. A number of research studies have been funded by the National Institute of Mental Health (NIMH) for the purpose of investigating possible genetic and biological causes as well as factors related to mental disorders and family history. According to researchers at NIMH, suicidal tendencies seem to have a stronger genetic basis than either schizophrenia or depression (Tugend, 1984a). Studies have also shown that genetic factors are associated with certain mental disorders—such as schizophrenia, affective disorders, and alcoholism—that are in turn significantly associated with suicidal behavior (Pfeffer, 1986; Tsuang, 1977).

BIOLOGICAL MARKERS FOR SUICIDE AND DEPRESSION

Biological markers are physical characteristics that have been found to be specifically related to the disorder in question (Puig-Antich, 1986). Studies by medical researchers have documented biological markers for suicide and depression in both children and adults that can be detected with medical tests. Medical researchers are hopeful that these biological markers may prove to be important clues for assessing suicidal risk in both adults and children.

Serotonin Deficiencies in Suicidal Individuals

Recent studies have suggested a strong relationship between suicide and low levels of serotonin in the brain. Serotonin, one of many neurotransmitters that control the activity of brain cells, is instrumental in controlling mood and emotion.

The current research on serotonin was sparked by a finding by the staff of the Karolinska Institute in Stockholm, Sweden (Asberg, Traskman, & Thoren, 1976). Asberg and her colleagues found that, of a group of depressed patients who had lower than normal levels of a serotonin metabolic product (5-hydroxyindoleacetic acid [5-HIAA]), 40% had attempted suicide. Among depressed patients with normal levels of 5-HIAA the suicide rate was 15%. Further, the attempts by the low 5-HIAA group were more serious and violent, such as using firearms and jumping from buildings, than those by the other patients, who had unsuccessfully attempted suicide by overdosing with drugs.

Other investigations have confirmed the link between suicide and low serotonin levels (Brown et al., 1982; Ninan et al., 1984). Researchers now generally agree that serotonin deficiency occurs in individuals who are prone to impulsive violence; and when these individuals are also depressed, they are more likely to commit suicide. Serotonin deficiency and depression together appear to increase the risk of suicide to a greater degree than does either factor alone, but there is no proof that lower serotonin levels are either a cause or effect of depression or impulsive behavior.

According to a researcher in psychopharmocology, the tendency toward low levels of serotonin in the brain may be hereditary, but the imbalance can be corrected with certain antidepressant drugs, which could serve to reduce suicidal behavior in susceptible teenagers (Mann, cited in "Heredity," 1987, p. 3A). A problem lies, however, in the identification of youngsters at risk; the only test for detecting serotonin levels is a spinal tap, which is both painful and expensive.

Birth Trauma Associated with Later Suicide

Some researchers have studied the association of adolescent suicides and risk factors that were apparent at birth. Researchers from Brown University compared the birth records of 52 Rhode Island adolescents who committed suicide between 1975 and 1983 with the birth records of carefully matched controls who were born in the same hospital at about the same times (Salk, Lipsitt, Sturner, Reilly, & Levat, 1985). The suicide group rated at least three times higher than the control group on three birth traumas—respiratory distress lasting for more than 1 hour after birth, no medical care in the first 20 weeks of pregnancy, and chronic disease in the mother. These researchers have cautioned against assuming a cause-and-effect relationship; they concluded that these risk factors may be symptomatic of, or may exacerbate, other conditions that may make a child vulnerable to suicide.

PSYCHIATRIC DISORDERS

The presence of a psychiatric disorder is one of the most important factors related to suicide risk in children and adolescents. Psychiatric disorders have often been reported in studies of completed suicide (Cosand et al., 1982; Garfinkel & Golumbek, 1974; Jan-Tausch, 1964; Shaffer, 1974; Toolan, 1962). According to Garfinkel (cited in Strother, 1986), suicide in children and youth who do not have psychiatric disorders is extremely rare.

Depression and Suicidal Behavior

A number of studies have confirmed that children and adolescents with depressive disorder are at high risk for suicidal behavior (Carlson & Cantwell, 1982; Cohen-Sandler et al., 1982; Dyer & Kreitman, 1984; Garfinkel & Golumbek, 1974; Mattson, Seese, & Hawkins, 1969; Pfeffer, 1984; Pfeffer, Conte, Plutchik, & Jerrett, 1979, 1980; Pfeffer & Plutchick, 1982; Pfeffer, Zuckerman, Plutchik, & Mizruchi, 1984; Robbins & Alessi, 1985; Shaffer, 1974; Toolan, 1978). Depression has also been found to be significantly more severe among suicidal children than among nonsuicidal children (Carlson & Cantwell, 1982; Pfeffer, Zuckerman et al., 1984).

Depression in Psychiatric Patients

In studies of children who were psychiatric inpatients and outpatients, significant relationships were found between depression and suicidal attempts, threats, and ideation (Pfeffer, Conte, et al., 1979, 1980; Pfeffer & Plutchik, 1982). Mattson et al. (1969) found that 40% of suicidal children referred for psychiatric emergency had previously shown signs of depression for at least 1 month.

Depression and Other Behavioral Disorders

Relationships have also been found between major depression and conduct disorder (Puig-Antich, 1982) and between major depression and separation anxiety (Geller, Chestnut, Miller, Price, & Yates, 1985). Because of these relationships, authorities often suggest that a child referred to a mental health professional for any type of psychiatric disorder should also be evaluated for depression and suicidal tendencies (Pfeffer, 1986).

Relationship Between Hopelessness and Depression

In a 5- to 10-year follow-up study of 207 patients who were previously hospitalized because of suicidal ideation (but who had not at that time attempted suicide), a significant relationship was found between hopelessness and later suicide (Beck, Steer, Kovacs, & Garrison, 1985). These researchers administered three instruments—the Beck Depression Inventory, the Hopelessness Scale, and the Scale for Suicide Ideation—to each patient at the time of admission to the hospital. Of the 207 patients, 34 (16.4%) later died, of which 14 (6.9%) had committed suicide. Scores on the Hopelessness Scale were the only scores that significantly differentiated between the patients who committed suicide and those who did not.

In children ages 8 to 13 years, suicidal risk has been found to be more highly correlated with the degree of hopelessness than with the severity of depression (Kazdin, French, Unis, Esveldt-Dawson, & Sherick, 1983). Kazdin et al. further found that (a) hopelessness was associated with both depression and low self-esteem and (b) relationships between depression, hopelessness, and suicidal behavior are the same for children and adults.

According to Maris (1981), chronic, repeated depressions tend to breed suicidal hopelessness. Hopelessness may be the final stage of depression that precedes suicidal behavior (Dyer & Kreitman, 1984; Sheras, 1983).

Depression in Young Children

Although depression was once considered to be an affliction of adults or adolescents, it is now evident that even very young children can develop this disorder. It has been estimated that approximately 2% of children ages 6 to 12 may suffer from serious depression (Ambrosini, cited in Conrad, 1986). Other reports of the prevalence of depression in young children have ranged from 1.8% in the general population (Kashani, McGee, et al., 1983) to 23% in orthopedic inpatients (Kashani, Venske, et al., 1981).

DRUG AND ALCOHOL ABUSE

Drug and alcohol use and abuse are powerful predictors of suicidal behavior in young people (Fowler, Rich, & Young, 1986; Hart & Keidel, 1979; Headlam, Goldsmith, Hanenson, & Rauh, 1979; Maris, 1981; Robbins & Alessi, 1985; Shaffer, 1974; "Suicide, Part 1," 1986). The American Academy of Pediatrics (cited in Mason, 1985) has reported an even higher percentage—that 70% of adolescent suicide victims have alcohol in their systems. Preliminary data from a recent study by Shaffer (1985) revealed that approximately half of a group of youngsters who had committed suicide were known to have abused drugs or alcohol. In an earlier study, Shaffer (1974) found that two of the three children in his study whose suicides appeared to be unplanned were intoxicated at the time.

It has also been reported that young people who committed suicide with firearms were five times more likely to have been drinking than those who used other means ("Accidents," 1987). The use of these more lethal means serves to make rescue less possible. Suicidal acts often occur during a drinking binge ("Suicide, Part 1," 1986). In periodic alcoholics, suicide is most apt to occur toward the end of a binge and is usually associated with feelings of guilt and self-reproach, which lower the victim's defenses against self-destructive behavior (Litman, 1970). According to many authorities, alcoholics are likely to become depressed when drinking, while losing the inhibitions that keep them from acting impulsively.

According to Litman (1970), about 5% of any group of alcoholics may be expected to commit suicide. Maris (1981) has proposed an even higher estimate of 7-21%.

Suicide Attempts Among Substance Abusers

Adolescents account for approximately 20% of the drug-related suicide attempts seen in hospital emergency rooms, and as many as 80% of adolescent suicide attempters are under the influence of alcohol at the time of the attempt (American Psychiatric Association, 1985). Golumbek and Garfinkel (1983) reported drug use in over one-third of a group of adolescents who attempted suicide, as compared with only 5% of a control group.

Study by National Institute on Drug Abuse

A large-scale longitudinal study of clients being treated for drug abuse (National Institute on Drug Abuse, 1985) found high rates of suicidal behavior and depression among clients under the age of 21. Suicidal thoughts and attempts were reported by all types of drug users, as were a wide array of other medical, social, legal, family, and job or school problems that were drug related. Many clients from groups generally considered to be at low risk, such as young Black males, reported suicidal symptoms. This study also revealed that clients who were highly involved in the drug use network—in drug sales or with friends who were drug users—were more likely to attempt suicide than those who avoided the network.

Drug Abuse As a Suicide Equivalent

Drug abuse itself may be a "suicide equivalent" (Hawton, 1986, p.

82), especially when the drugs used are dangerous and the danger is clearly understood by the adolescent. The same problems that lead a person to abuse drugs and alcohol may also lead him to kill himself (Greuling & DeBlassie, 1980). It is not easy, however, to distinguish between a deliberate self-poisoning and an accidental overdose.

Use of Legal Drugs in Suicides and Attempts

According to Hawton and Goldacre (1982), young people who attempt suicide by ingesting legal drugs are usually acting impulsively, so the drugs used are those that are readily available, such as analgesics (aspirin and acetaminophen) and psychotropics. Although most attempts by ingesting legal drugs are relatively nonlethal (Barter, Swaback, & Todd, 1968; Hawton, Cole, O'Grady, & Osborn, 1982), with some legal drugs there is serious risk of respiratory depression and death (Hawton, 1986). In both the United States and the United Kingdom, there has been a recent large increase in the number of overdoses of acetaminophen (Tylenol), which has the potential for causing a delayed death from liver damage (Davidson & Eastman, 1966; Hawton, 1986; Rumack, 1983).

FAMILY PROBLEMS ASSOCIATED WITH SUICIDAL BEHAVIOR

Family factors generally associated with suicidal behavior in children and adolescents include a family history of suicidal behavior, psychiatric illness, or substance abuse; loss of a parent through death, divorce, or separation; abuse, violence, and neglect; and other major family stresses. Recent research has also confirmed the association of some of these risk factors with the presence of depression and other psychiatric disorders in young people.

Family History of Suicidal Behavior

Several researchers have reported an association between children's suicidal behavior and a family history of suicidal behavior (Carlson & Cantwell, 1982; Garfinkel, Froese, & Hood, 1982; Myers, Burke, & McCauley, 1985; Pfeffer, 1980; Pfeffer, Zuckerman, et al., 1984). According to authorities at NIMH, a family history of suicide increases the suicide risk eightfold among young people ages 15 to 24 (Silver, 1985). It may be that children model the behaviors and attitudes of their parents and siblings, including familial traits associated with suicide, such as depression, alcoholism, and hopelessness, as well as the actual suicidal act (Maris, 1981; Shaffer, 1974; Silver, 1985).

Family History of Psychiatric Illness

A history of psychiatric disorders in the family—such as parental psychopathology and substance abuse—has often been found to be related to suicidal behavior in children and youth (Carlson & Cantwell, 1982; Cohen-Sandler et al., 1982; Garfinkel, Froese, & Hood, 1982; Green, 1978; Murphy & Wetzel, 1982; Tishler & McKenry, 1982). In a comparison of young people who had attempted suicide with a control group of nonsuicidal youth, Garfinkel, Froese and Hood (1982) found that 52% of the attempters but only 16% of the nonsuicidal group had a history of family psychiatric disorder. Tishler and McKenry (1982) found fathers of suicide attempters to be significantly more depressed, to consume significantly more alcohol, and to have significantly lower self-esteem than fathers of nonattempters. Litman and Diller (1985) compared the histories of persons ages 21 or younger with those of comparable living peers who were friends of the victims. Family problems such as a depressed parent or a suicidal parent were more prevalent among the victims.

Loss and Separation

The loss of one or both parents through death, divorce, or separation has often been cited as a factor in the suicidal behavior of young people (Blaine & Carmen, 1968; Cohen-Sandler et al., 1982; Dorpat, Jackson, & Ripley, 1965; Margolin & Teicher, 1968; Morrison & Collier, 1969; Murphy & Wetzel, 1982; Schneer, Kay, & Brozovsky, 1961; Shaffer, 1974; Tishler, McKenry, & Morgan, 1981; Wenz, 1979). Jacobs and Teicher (1967) found not only repetitive experiences of separation and loss throughout the lives of suicidal adolescents, but also escalation of these problems occurring immediately before the suicidal acts. Barter et al. (1968) compared adolescents who made repeated attempts at suicide with those who made only one attempt. Those not living with their families and those who had experienced an earlier parental loss were most likely to show a recurrence of suicidal behavior.

Barter et al. further noted a persistent threat of loss due to parental marital problems and frequent discussion of divorce in the families of suicidal youth. Richman (1986) has also found the threat of loss to be a major factor, noting that in the families of suicidal individuals "the threat of loss hangs heavy in the air " (p. 6).

Abuse, Violence, and Neglect

Family patterns of neglectful, violent, and abusive behavior have often been associated with suicidal behavior in both children and adolescents (Adams-Tucker, 1982; Anderson, 1981; Bible & French, 1979; Lucianowicz, 1968; Myers et al., 1985; Pfeffer, 1986; Pfeffer, Conte, et al., 1979; Schneer et al., 1961; Taylor & Stansfield, 1984; Tuckman & Connon, 1962). Kosky (1983) reported child abuse in 60% of a group of children who had attempted suicide, as compared with 4% of a group of psychiatrically ill children who were not suicidal. Adams-Tucker (1982) found suicidal and self-destructive behavior to be the most common psychiatric disturbance among sexually abused children.

Henry and Short (1954) noted that punitive child-rearing practices were a common factor in families of suicidal youth. According to these authors, children who are subjected to severe punishment at the hands of their parents tend to vent their frustrations upon themselves, both during childhood and later, when they are frustrated as adults. Green (1978) found that self-destructive actions by violently abused children were often precipitated by these children being beaten by their parents.

Other Family Stressors

Studies of suicidal children and adolescents have often reported that the youngsters were subjected to major stresses, including hospitalizations, frequent changes in home and school, remarriages of parents, incarcerations of parents for legal or psychiatric reasons, poor peer or sibling relationships, siblings leaving home, unreasonable expectations by parents, and family financial problems (Ackerly, 1967; Jacobziner, 1965; Lucianowicz, 1968; Myers et al., 1985; Otto, 1972; Schrut, 1964; Teicher & Jacobs, 1966; Toolan, 1978). Tuckman and Connon (1962) described poor home conditions, family disorganization, and parental disharmony in the families of suicidal youth. In a 5-year study of student suicide, depression, and crisis, Hendin (1975a, 1975b) found serious family disturbances to be related to suicidal behavior in both high school and college students. Cohen-Sandler et al. (1982) investigated differences between suicidal and nonsuicidal children in a sample of psychiatric patients. They found that the suicidal children had not only experienced greater stress from disruptive family events, but that the amount of stress had increased as the children grew older.

ENVIRONMENTAL AND SOCIOCULTURAL FACTORS

The increases in the rates of youth suicide over the past decade have often been attributed to a number of sociocultural and environmental factors such as the declining influence of religion; the breakdown in the nuclear family unit; the increased mobility of young people; the blurring of sex roles; the increase in violence; increasing pressure on young people to achieve; the rise in the cost of higher education; unemployment; isolation; alienation; contagion; and many other problems in the home, school, and community. According to Shaffer and Fisher (1981), such factors could operate by either enhancing a predisposition to suicidal behavior or by weakening suicide-inhibiting factors (or both). Some of these factors that are most often mentioned in the literature are briefly discussed here.

Social Acceptance of Suicidal Behavior

Shaffer (1986) has suggested that there are cultural and environmental factors that now permit expression of depression and aggression that was previously taboo. As an example, he has cited the legitimizing of suicidal behavior in certain societies—that suicide was once considered a profane and illegal act but is now perceived as a manifestation of mental illness.

Effect of Religion

Havighurst (1969) has pointed to the low rates of suicide in Muslim and Catholic countries as evidence that religion, or the lack of same, is a factor in suicidal behavior. Another explanation for the variance in rates, according to Havighurst, is the way people in a given society learn to cope with aggression, which may be directed inward (against the self) or outward (against others).

Violence and Suicide

Hendin (1982) has proposed a direct connection between violence and suicide.

> All forms of psychosocial pathology tend to correlate with each other, if only for the simple reason that an individual who is in distress is likely to manifest this distress in more than one way. The early life disturbances seen in individuals who later become suicidal violent, or alcoholic lead . . . to a vulnerability that often does not appear to be specifically directed to one form of disorder. (pp. 86–87)

Hendin has also suggested that the sociocultural acceptance of guns in the United States is a factor in their use as a means of committing suicide.

According to Gastil (1971), there is a regional culture of violence (specifically in the southern United States), with the availability of weapons and a knowledge of how to use them as contributing factors. Marks and Abernathy (1974) further found that in the southern United States, where guns are most accepted as part of the household effects, and where children may often be introduced to firearms by their parents, guns were used to commit suicide more frequently than in other parts of the country.

SOCIAL ISOLATION

Many authorities have suggested that isolation places young people at risk for suicidal behavior. Jan-Tausch (1964) found that many completed suicides took place after a period of absence from school. Other data from this study indicated that the victims lacked friends and that they did not participate in extracurricular activities. Absence from school has also been found to be associated with suicide attempts (Stanley & Barter, 1970; Teicher & Jacobs, 1966). Stanley and Barter further noted that the best predictor for a positive outcome after a student's suicide attempt was a return to school followed by regular attendance.

In Shaffer's study (1974), 12 of the 30 subjects were not at school the day before they died. Of that number, three were chronic school refusers, four were on vacation (the suicide occurring during a school holiday), and five were truant (Shaffer & Fisher, 1981). Shaffer and Fisher suggested that emotional problems may have contributed to the refusers' and truants' being away from school, but that being out of the school environment apparently renders children more vulnerable to suicide.

In 1962, Litman (cited in Peck, 1968) conducted a study of adolescent suicides and found that the male victims, in particular, were often described as quiet, obedient, studious, moody, and socially isolated. Jan-Tausch (1964) found that young suicide victims lacked friends and that they did not participate in extracurricular activities. Peck and Schrut (1971) found that college students who committed suicide were isolated and unlikely to communicate their needs for help. These and other similar studies prompted the staff of the Los Angeles Suicide Prevention Center to devise the category of "loner" for one type of youngster who is at risk for committing suicide (Peck, 1985).

The Loner

The loner, according to Peck (1985), is more likely to be male than female and White than nonWhite. He frequently has a history, beginning in the early teens, of spending much of his spare time alone, of having poor interpersonal relationships with peers and adults, and of feeling lonely and isolated much of the time. His friendships are superficial, and he rarely has a close friend in whom to confide.

Richman (1986) has suggested, however, that the isolated, schizoid individual who is comfortable with being alone is not at risk for suicide. It is rather the social isolation of a young person who longs for acceptance that is deadly.

Lack of Meaningful Social Relationships

The isolation associated with suicidal behavior is often social or psychological rather than geographical. A child who is rejected or unaccepted by his peers can be isolated in a crowded classroom. The critical factor is not physical distance, but rather the degree to which the youngster is unable to form relationships with peers and adults.

Barter et al. (1968) found a lack of social resources to be related to suicidal behavior in young people. Teicher and Jacobs (1966) have proposed that suicidal youth encounter a long history of problems that serve to progressively isolate them from meaningful social relationships. According to these authors, this isolation not only constitutes the problem, but also serves to preclude any possibility of solving it.

Maris (1981) found that suicidal people may not be physically isolated from others. They are instead often involved in self-destructive interpersonal relationships that may lead them to either cut themselves off from life itself or to use nonlethal suicide attempts to try to change the quality of life. It is the nature of their relationships (rather than the lack of them) that contributes to suicidal behavior.

Isolation is also considered to be a warning sign of imminent suicidal behavior. Suicidal youngsters often withdraw from extracurricular activities, drop out of school, or isolate themselves from friends and family.

Alienation

Several studies have reported evidence of alienation as a factor related to suicidal behavior in young people. "Suicide is the ultimate expression of alienation. It is . . . a deficiency disease, a deficiency of social connections" (Eisenberg, 1980, p. 319). Jacobs and Teicher

(1967) found that young people who had attempted suicide were more likely to be alienated from their parents than were nonsuicidal controls, whether or not they came from a broken home. R. E. Gould (1965) and Schrut (1964) reported evidence of parental hostility, resentment, and rejection toward youngsters who later became suicidal. According to Sabbath (1969), an important factor in a child's suicidal behavior is the parent's conscious or unconscious wish to be rid of him. The "expendable child" becomes suicidal when he perceives, after years of verbal and nonverbal interactions with family members, that he is no longer needed or tolerated. Jourard (1969) referred to this situation as "the invitation to die."

Klagsbrun (cited in Ring, 1984) has suggested that alienation from peers often results from the child's poor "fit" within the family. "There is a high correlation between having a sense of success and belonging at home and being a successful peer group member . . . . The real misfit at home is very often on the periphery of the gang, a misfit there, too " (p. 2).

According to Richman (1986), the most painful and unbearable situation occurs when alienation extends even beyond the family and the peer group. "When alienation encompasses the family and the social world, extends to the physical universe and even the spiritual realm, . . . there is indeed no refuge. The separation is complete, the despair unresolvable, unless hope can be restored" (p. 134).

HOMOSEXUALITY AS A RISK FACTOR

It is generally accepted that homosexual youth are at risk of becoming isolated or alienated from family and peers (Bell & Weinberg, 1978; Berlin, 1979). There is a relative paucity, however, of data from well-designed studies regarding the relationship of suicidal behavior and homosexuality in young people. Sagher and Robins (1971) compared information regarding 89 male and 57 female homosexuals with 78 male and female heterosexual controls. The homosexuals exhibited more depression, had more suicide attempts, and had abused alcohol more often than did the heterosexuals. Roesler and Deisher (1972) interviewed 60 young male homosexuals whose ages ranged from 16 to 22 years and found that 48% had sought psychiatric assistance and 31% had made a serious suicide attempt.

RISK FACTORS RELATED TO LEARNING AND COGNITION

Many authorities have suggested that mere knowledge of suicide contributes to an individual's being at risk of suicidal behavior (Cain, 1972). Young people who have attempted suicide are more likely than nonattempters to know and be close to others who have talked about suicide or exhibited suicidal behavior (Kreitman, Smith, & Tan, 1970; Tishler & McKenry, 1982). Knowledge of a previous suicide might simply validate suicide as an option that has already been considered, or it may present suicide as a possibility that might otherwise never have been considered.

REINFORCEMENT OF SUICIDAL BEHAVIOR

Suicidal behavior, together with the depressive components associated with it, can be reinforced if desired changes occur in the environment (Frederick, 1978, 1985; Frederick & Resnick, 1971). Frederick (1985) has suggested that if self-destructive acts result in a reduction in tension, the likelihood of their recurrence is increased markedly, particularly when situations similar to those that led to the initial tension state recur.

Vicarious reinforcement of suicidal behavior can also occur when a young person realizes that a great deal of attention has been given to a suicide victim or to a person who has made a suicide attempt. This reinforcement is likely an important factor in suicide contagion.

REHEARSAL OF SUICIDAL BEHAVIOR

Litman (1970) has discussed the concepts of rehearsal and reinforcement as important to the crystallization of a suicide plan. According to Litman, thoughts of suicide begin as fantasy for the purpose of resolving crises and providing temporary relief during times of tension. From such thoughts, the fantasies evolve gradually into a suicide plan, which is strengthened by wishes, memories, and fantasies. The plan is further reinforced by repetitions in imagination, by threats and promises, and by preliminary actions, such as the selection or acquisition of a weapon. The suicide plan then takes on the qualities of an incomplete or interrupted act. Such acts, according to Litman, have "an autonomous momentum toward completion" (1970, p. 303).

THE CHILD'S CONCEPT OF DEATH AS REVERSIBLE

The relationship between the young child's concept of death and self-destructive behavior has been the subject of considerable discussion (Baechler, 1979; de Catanzaro, 1981; Frederick, 1978; Koocher, 1973; Pfeffer, 1986; Winn & Halla, 1966). Paradoxically, the concept of death as temporary has been cited both as a risk factor for suicide and as a reason for its infrequency in young children.

Baechler (1979) found that, of 165 cases of suicide recorded at a Paris hospital, the youngest was 7. He concluded that between the ages of 7 and 12 or 13, suicide is rare but does exist, and that children seldom have a clear perception of death before the age of 10. Other researchers have reported that children as old as 13 still believe that death is reversible (Freud & Burlingham, 1944; McIntyre & Angle, 1973; Nagy, 1948; Schilder & Wechsler, 1934). Koocher (1973) has linked children's concepts of death to Piagetian stages of cognition. None of his subjects who had attained the stage of concrete or formal operations still believed in the reversibility of death, but he found preoperational thought in some 11-year-old children.

According to Baechler, the "meaningful types of suicide—escape, grief, and punishment" (1979, p. 287) are not prevalent among young children. Shaffer and Fisher (1981) have also suggested that some degree of cognitive maturity is required before a child can succumb to despair and hopelessness. On the other hand, believing death to be reversible may also serve to reduce constraints on suicidal behavior. Young children often see films and cartoons in which their heroes and heroines "die," only to live again in the next movie. There have been a number of reports of the deaths of young children after they had watched movies or television programs in which a character was killed—by himself or others. Such deaths are generally considered to be accidental, since the children could not have understood the full consequences of their actions.

Baechler recognized that children's ignorance about death may put them in dangerous and lethal situations without their realizing it.

> These cases should be regarded as accidents, although the behavior may foreshadow a meaningful type of suicide. Children may court death, and do it so well that they succeed; they may throw themselves out of the window to avenge themselves after reprimands, etc. (1979, p. 287)

Shaffer (1974) found evidence of careful and intelligent planning by many of the suicide victims in his study. He suggested that this ability to plan ahead, necessary to suicidal purpose, is not common until later childhood. Suicidal intent, however, has been documented in very young children, as discussed in Chapter 5 (Rosenthal & Rosenthal, 1984).

RECKLESSNESS AND CARELESSNESS AS RISK FACTORS

In addition to the self-killings of young children who do not understand the finality of death, there are other deaths resulting from self-destructive behavior that may not be consciously suicidal (Litman, 1980). According to Shneidman and Mandelkorn (1970), some people, who want to die but have not reached the state at which they will act consciously on this desire, begin to live more carelessly and unconsciously put themselves in peril. An individual who is chronically ill may stop taking life-saving medicine; a depressed student may drive recklessly. "Fate will make the crucial decision, but they are giving death the edge" (p. 140). Farberow (1980) has referred to such behaviors as "unconscious suicidal tendencies" or "indirect self-destructive behavior" (p. 16). He includes the following, among others, in that category: alcohol or drug addiction, smoking, hyperobesity, rioting, repeated accidents, delinquency, Russian roulette, skydiving, violent contact sports, stunt performing, and motorcycle racing. According to the commonly used classification of deaths, these cases may be called "subintentioned deaths" (Shneidman & Mandelkorn, p. 139).

One form of reckless behavior may often result in death that is classified as homicide. In victim-precipitated homicide (Wolfgang, 1958, 1959), the victim plays a conscious or subconscious role, in that he places himself in an extremely vulnerable position and encourages someone else to kill him, such as the case in which the victim walks alone late at night in a high-risk neighborhood. In a study of 300 homicidal deaths, Wolfgang classified 26% as falling in this category.

SUMMARY

Some of the more important risk factors found to be associated with youth suicide are the following:

1. Previous suicidal behavior.
2. A personal history of psychiatric disorder or substance abuse.
3. A family history of suicide, psychiatric disorder, substance abuse, or disorganization.
4. The loss of a parent through death, divorce, or separation.
5. Abuse, violence, or neglect.

6. Social isolation and alienation.

7. Knowledge of suicide.

These and other risk factors related to suicidal behavior in children and adolescents have been discussed previously. Events that may precipitate suicidal actions are discussed in the next chapter.

8. Events That Precipitate Suicidal Behavior

A great number of stressful situations or events have the potential for precipitating suicidal behavior in children and adolescents. Among the most common are losses or disappointments resulting from conflicts with family members, disruptions of relationships with girlfriends or boyfriends, and problems at school (Golumbek & Garfinkel, 1983; Hawton & O'Grady, 1982; Jacobziner, 1965; Mattson et al., 1969; Peck, 1985).

The presence of a situational crisis, as discussed in the section on assessment, is one of the important warning signs of potential suicide. The following situations and events are commonly cited as possible precipitants of suicidal behavior in children and adolescents:

1. Death of a family member, friend, or acquaintance (particularly if by suicide).
2. Loss or disruption of a romantic relationship or friendship.
3. Divorce, separation, or remarriage of parents.
4. Loss of a treasured activity, object, or opportunity.
5. Fear of punishment in the home, school, or community.
6. Debilitating injury or illness.
7. Physical, sexual, or psychological abuse.
8. Pregnancy, abortion, or the birth of a child.
9. Loss of social status (or unwanted publicity).
10. Poor academic achievement (or dropping out of school).
11. Loss of employment—by self or parent.
12. Change (usually a decrease) in financial resources.
13. Fight or argument with loved one.
14. Death or loss of a pet.
15. Marriage (or permanent departure from home) of a sibling.

16. Concerns about sexuality (or being recognized as homosexual).
17. Being arrested (or undetected involvement in illegal activity).
18. Embarrassment about physical appearance.
19. Intoxication.
20. Bringing harm to a friend or family member.
21. Humiliation (especially in the presence of family or peers).

Although many of these problems or events may seem trivial to an adult, to a young person they may loom as insurmountable. There is increased danger when several of these events occur at the same time or when one causes another to happen.

It is evident that almost every child may be subjected to one or more of these problems. Most children survive; some are more fragile. Shaffer (1974) found the following factors to be precipitants of suicide in his sample of children and adolescents: (a) disciplinary crisis, (b) fight or dispute with peers, (c) date within 2 weeks of birthday, (d) dispute with parent, (e) interaction with psychotic parent, (f) being dropped from a school team, and (g) fantasy models. Two suicides were apparently triggered by reading material (fantasy model)—one by reports of the suicide of a public figure, which was mentioned in the suicide note, and one by a novel (in which a teenage boy commits suicide), which was found near the child's body. Seven of the 30 children died within 2 weeks of their birthdays. During the 24 hours immediately preceding their deaths, 4 had been involved in fights and 2 had run away from home.

A situation that points to the need for supervision, particularly of children who are not attending school, was evident in those cases in which children had gassed themselves with carbon monoxide. Of the 13 victims who used this method, 10 were alone at home at the time.

FEAR OF PUNISHMENT

The most common precipitating event, noted by Shaffer (1974), was a disciplinary crisis, which accounted for 36% of the cases in his study. One half of the disciplinary crises were situations in which the child had been truant or had committed some other antisocial act of which the parents were not yet aware. In the remaining cases, the child was expecting punishment from either the school or the court (Shaffer & Fisher, 1981). Shaffer also found that children who killed themselves during or after a disciplinary crisis were less likely than others to have made previous threats or attempts (Shaffer & Fisher, 1981). In such cases, the disciplinary crisis itself may be the only apparent warning sign.

The 10-year-old was worried about bringing home bad grades for the third consecutive time, so he left his report card at school. His father, suspicious when the other children brought home their cards, went to school, picked up the report card, and told the boy that they were going to have a discussion about it when he returned from shopping. During the half hour that his father was gone, the boy shot himself to death. He had told his brother and sister that he couldn't stand the idea of a whipping.

An 8-year-old boy was accused of stealing $4 from his teacher's purse. According to his family, he became extremely depressed over the accusation. He used his belt to hang himself from his bunk bed.

Unknown Consequences

In a current study, Shaffer (cited in Ritter, 1988) has again found that the most common trigger event for suicide among teenagers was getting into trouble at school, with the police, or with the family, and not knowing what the consequences would be. He has suggested that these youngsters were probably highly anxious, bordering on being terrified, when they killed themselves.

Being Arrested

Suicidal behavior in young people who have been arrested or who are otherwise in trouble with the law has been documented in several studies (Breed, 1970; Maris, 1969; Sathyavathi, 1975).

In a small town in Florida, an adolescent boy, who had previously been guilty of a minor infraction of the law, had been warned by the judge, who was also a family friend, that if he was ever arrested again, he would be jailed. The judge's intention was to frighten the youngster into obeying the law. At a later date, upon having a minor traffic accident, the youngster ran from the scene and shot himself to death. He left a suicide note, in which he apologized for his actions and explained that he would rather die than go to jail, where he would be raped by the other prisoners.

LITERATURE, FILMS, AND OTHER MEDIA

In Shaffer's (1974) study, two of the suicides appeared to be precipitated by reading materials. Other fantasy models, as further discussed in the next chapter, may include movies, television programs, plays, games, and music.

Two teenage girls shared a bottle of champagne and wrote letters to their families about how happy they were going to be. They then took a shotgun and killed themselves. In their letters they cited song lyrics from rock music. They died 2 days after the airing of a television movie about the suicide of a teenaged boy.

There have been a number of reports in the newspapers and on television of suicides (and homicides) that were apparently precipitated by the involvement of children and adolescents in violent role-playing activities such as the game "Dungeons and Dragons." This game has been cited as a factor in reports of more than 30 deaths of young people across the continent, including at least 9 suicides, within the 5-year period from 1980 to 1985 (Guetzloe, 1987; Shoaff, 1985).

One of the victims, a 16-year-old boy, had played the game in the gifted and talented program at his high school in Virginia for about 6 months before his death. As part of the game, a fellow player (the "Dungeon Master") placed a curse on the character he had assumed in the game. A few hours later, the boy shot himself and died at his home. His parents filed a lawsuit against the manufacturers of the game and against the two teachers who had instructed him in how to play. The suit was later dismissed, but the parents have organized Bothered About Dungeons and Dragons (BADD), a group of parents, physicians, lawyers, and mental health professionals that are concerned about the effects of this game and other violent role-playing on impressionable children and youth (Pulling, personal communication, 1985).

SCHOOL PROBLEMS

Many reports of suicidal behavior have cited school problems as precipitating events. According to Garfinkel (cited in Anderson, 1986), 3 of the 10 leading causes of stress in adolescents are school based (problems with academics, peers, and teachers); and 1 in 10 suicide attempts is related to a crisis at school. Poor academic achievement, difficulties in relationships with peers or teachers, truancy, dropping out, and the desire to leave school have been noted in young people who made suicide attempts (Barter et al., 1968; Garfinkel, Froese, & Hood, 1982; Hawton, 1986; Otto, 1972).

Academic Pressure

Seiden (1966), in summarizing a study of suicides among university students, suggested that increasing pressure for academic achievement would lead to an increase in the suicide rate among the student population. Results of research have indicated that suicidal students are seldom satisfied with their grades, no matter how high they are (Klagsbrun, 1976). Further, a failure on a test may be perceived by an adolescent to be failure in life itself. A school problem is particularly devastating to a good student with high expectations for achievement.

> A 15-year-old honors student and Eagle Scout, known as a "quiet kind of guy," stood up at the end of his advanced literature class on a Thursday, pulled a handgun from his pocket and, without a word, shot himself in the head. He had been given a notice, which his parents were to sign, that he was not doing well in the class. He had the unsigned notice with him. He had also failed to turn in a paper that was due on Monday. According to friends, he had been laughing about that just before class.
>
> One classmate said that "he just had too much pressure," another that "he was one of those kids who's just got everything." The literature teacher said that, despite the fact that she had issued an academic warning, the boy was doing well in the class.

Embarrassment

There are many other school situations and events that have the potential for causing embarrassment and humiliation, which may in turn lead to suicidal behavior. The fear of being embarrassed at school because of poor physical appearance was apparently a precipitant in the following case.

> The scribbled note said, "I can't stand another day of school and especially another day without television." It was found next to the body of a lonely, overweight 13-year-old who had killed himself with a single shot to the head from his father's revolver.
>
> The boy had refused to go to his new school because he would have to shower with other students after physical education classes. He had shut himself in his room, letting no one in without permission, and had spent his days watching television, playing video games, and reading. He shot himself just hours after his father had removed the television from his room. His

father had told him he could have the television back when he returned to school. The boy had received the television from his father as a reward for earning a high average at his previous school.

Even more devastating is a problem with personal appearance that is complicated by teasing or scapegoating by classmates. In the following case, the teasing apparently contributed to not only the suicide of an overweight child but also the death of a classmate.

A 12-year-old who was frequently teased about being overweight pulled a gun from his gym bag and killed a classmate and himself in their seventh-grade history class. The boy had warned his best friend the week before to stay out of school because he was "going to shoot everyone." One of the students said that everyone teased the boy and "called him chubby." The principal said that the boy was an honor roll student—"quiet and reserved."

Change of School

A recent move to a new school or community has often been cited in the histories of student suicides. Leaving friends and classmates is a tremendous loss for a young person. A father's promotion to a new position, not at all an unusual situation in an upwardly mobile family, has the potential for creating a crisis for a child. A movement made necessary by a loss of financial status may be even more critical, as are changes in school made necessary by divorce and custody decisions. In the latter situation, the child has suffered not only the separation from a parent (which is in itself a crisis) but also the loss of the peer support group.

LOSS OF A LOVE RELATIONSHIP

A number of studies have documented the loss of a significant interpersonal relationship as a precipitating event in suicide attempts of young people (Barter et al., 1968; Finch & Poznanski, 1971; Wenz, 1979). Barter et al. found that 66% of suicide attempts followed a loss or threatened loss of a love relationship. An argument with a parent apparently precipitated 33% of the attempts, while others took place following a breakup or threatened breakup with a boyfriend or girlfriend. The disruption of a love affair, even between very young adolescents, is a serious crisis. Generally, if the separation is final, the risk is even more serious.

A 19-year-old college student, upset over the breakup of the couple's relationship, shot his ex-girlfriend to death in view of more than a dozen children and adults at a neighborhood swimming pool. He then shot and killed himself. He was an engineering major, described by neighbors as a good student and "a very calm person . . . quiet in a way."

SUICIDE WITHOUT EVIDENCE OF PRECIPITATING STRESS

Suicides may often occur in the absence of obvious precipitating events. Some suicides appear to be impulsive, occurring without any of the usual warning signs. In other cases, warning signs are apparent only immediately before the suicidal act, when parents, friends, and school personnel have very little time to intervene.

A high school student who climbed on a classroom stage and shot himself as a teacher and four classmates watched had been a good student and had shown no signs of suicidal distress. The 17-year-old, a drama student with a flair for jokes, killed himself after asking others in the classroom "heavy philosophical questions" about the meaning of life.

He had the lead in the school play. He walked into the drama classroom, sat on a stool on the stage, and began asking questions. According to the students, "it was his nature to fool around," so they didn't think his behavior was out of the ordinary. He then pulled a sawed-off shotgun from a briefcase, placed it against his temple, and pulled the trigger. He was pronounced dead at the scene.

One of his classmates said that the victim was "a real deep kind of guy." He kept his personal life to himself. He was further described by his friends as an intellectual who enjoyed playing "Dungeons and Dragons."

His mother had found the stock of the shotgun in his room after he had come home for lunch that day. According to both the mother and the school authorities, the boy showed none of the usual signs of potential suicide.

THE CHRONICALLY SUICIDAL

Children and youth who are seriously emotionally disturbed, who have a long history of serious problems, or who have a history of suicide attempts are also at risk of killing themselves in the absence of obvious trigger events. These youngsters, who have been called chronically suicidal, exhibit little or no precipitating stress prior to their suicidal actions (Peck, 1985).

SUMMARY

In conclusion, any number of stressful events may trigger suicidal behavior in young people. The preceding discussion has focused on those precipitating events that have been identified most often in research studies or news reports. It must be clearly understood, however, that many suicides of children and adolescents have occurred without warning—in the apparent absence of precipitating stress.

The problem of contagion is a phenomenon that could be categorized as either a risk factor related to learning or a precipitating event for suicidal behavior. Because of its singular importance, contagion is discussed separately in the next chapter.

9. Problem of Contagion

The contagious nature of youth suicide is a topic of considerable current debate among suicidologists, but it is not a recent phenomenon. In 1774, Johann Wolfgang von Goethe published a novel, *The Sorrows of Young Werther*, in which the hero, a gifted young man, shot himself to death. The book, which was widely read in Europe, was blamed for leading other young people to kill themselves, some by identical methods. Two hundred years later, Phillips proposed the term, "the Werther effect" to explain the influence of suggestion on suicide (1974, p. 340).

Durkheim (1897) did not believe that imitation played an important role in determining suicide rates, although he acknowledged that no other phenomenon was more readily contagious. There is some evidence, however, of temporary increases in suicide rates that seem to be the result of imitation.

Havighurst, in a discussion of education's responsibility in preventing youth suicide, cited both the rash of suicides following the publication of Goethe's novel and the following incident as examples of specific causes of "sharp, local increases" in suicide rates (1969, p. 57).

> More striking still is the outbreak of suicides on the Japanese volcano-island of Mihara-Yama. A girl of nineteen, Kiyoko Matsumoto, took a boat to this small island, about a 2-hour trip from Tokyo, climbed up the side of the mountain to the crater's edge, and threw herself in. This occurred in February 1933. The newspapers played it up. In the remaining 10 months of 1933, 143 people jumped into the crater. A steamship company established a thriving tourist business carrying sightseers to the island from Tokyo. In one particular day there were 6 completed suicides and 25 attempts. The next year, 1934, there were 167 suicides on the island. In 1935, the government took steps to screen passengers on the boat and stopped the suicide fad. (Havighurst, 1969, p. 57)

EFFECTS OF THE MEDIA

Several studies have shown that there is a significant relationship between media coverage of suicide and temporary increases in suicide rates, particularly among teenagers (Bollen & Phillips, 1982; Gould, M. S., & Shaffer, 1986; Phillips, 1974, 1979; Phillips & Carstensen, 1986). Phillips (1974) found that monthly suicide rates in the United States increased during the month of a front-page suicide story in the newspapers, that the increase was proportional to the amount of publicity accorded the story, and that the increase occurred mainly in the geographical areas receiving the publicity. Phillips (1979) also found a link between an increase in suicide rates and the suicide obituaries appearing on the front page of the *New York Times* during the period from 1948 to 1967. Bollen and Phillips (1982) further found that daily suicides increased significantly after (and not before) highly publicized suicide stories that appeared on television news programs and that the effect seemed to last for about 10 days.

Wasserman (1984) re-examined Phillips' 1979 data and found that the suicides of celebrities, particularly those in the entertainment field, appeared to be the trigger events. Following the deaths of actress Marilyn Monroe and comedian Freddie Prinze, suicides increased 12% and 18%, respectively, while the suicide of former U.S. Secretary of State James Forrestal was followed by only a 4% increase. Wasserman suggested that the factors involved in the increase may be either that people identify more closely with entertainment celebrities or that the suicides of these individuals receive more media coverage. Shaffer & Fisher (1981) have suggested that the suicidal death of a public figure may also serve to reduce social constraints on this type of behavior.

Phillips and Carstensen (1986), in a review of 12,585 teenage suicides reported between 1973 and 1979, found that the national rate of suicide among teenagers rises significantly just after television news or feature stories about suicide, with the increase being proportional to the amount of network coverage. The effect was much greater for teenagers than for adults and greater for females than for males. The increase was just as great after general information or feature stories as after reports of a specific suicide. After an assessment of six alternative explanations for the findings, the researchers have concluded that publicized television stories about suicide trigger additional suicides. The authors have suggested that educators, journalists, and policy makers may wish to consider reducing public exposure to stories about suicide.

A study by M. S. Gould and Shaffer (1986), which focused on the greater New York area, found that suicide and suicide attempts increased significantly during the 2-week periods following several television movies about suicide. The movies in question were made specifically for television and were broadcast during the period from October 1984 through February 1985.

> The first movie . . . was an after-school special . . . which depicted two male high-school students who made a suicide pact. One of them eventually committed suicide by driving his car off a cliff. The second film . . . depicted a 17-year-old male high-school student who committed suicide after several interpersonal crises. Most of the film focused on the reactions of the surviving family members. The third movie . . . dealt with a teenager's efforts to stop his father's suicide. The fourth . . . was a story of a teenage boy and girl who jointly committed suicide. (Gould, M. S., & Shaffer, 1986, p. 690)

Professional advisers had assisted in the production of all of the films, which were accompanied by educational and preventive materials made available to local network affiliates for distribution. The program with the most extensive resources—widely distributed scripts and teacher's guides, onscreen displays of local suicide hotline numbers, and a follow-up television message—was the only one of the four films not followed by a completed suicide in the New York area. After the other three films, the rates for both suicides and attempts among teenagers in that geographical area rose significantly.

M. S. Gould and Shaffer (1986) explored alternative explanations for the findings, such as referral bias among parents or increased awareness of suicide on the part of medical examiners or hospital personnel, but found that these explanations were unlikely to account for the increases in attempted and completed suicides. Although they could not determine, with one exception, whether the suicidal youngsters had actually seen the films, the researchers concluded that television broadcasts of fictional stories about suicide may lead to imitative behavior among teenagers.

> At present, it is impossible to determine conclusively whether it was the content of the films . . ., the context of the broadcasts . . ., or both that either increased or diminished suicidal behavior. It seems advisable to develop a research strategy to identify the components of broadcasts that diminish suicidal behavior, if there are any, and those that encourage it. This is a matter of some urgency, because the presumptive evidence suggests that fictional presentations of suicide may have a lethal effect. (Gould, M. S., & Shaffer, 1986, p. 693)

Phillips and Paight (1987) replicated the M. S. Gould and Shaffer study in the states of California and Pennsylvania and found no significant effect for the same movies. In yet another replication and expansion of the original study, M. S. Gould, Shaffer, and Kleinman (1988) found a significant excess of suicides following the broadcasts of fictional stories in the New York and Cleveland regions, but not in the Dallas or Los Angeles areas. According to M. S. Gould et al., both sets of results might be explained by an interaction between the locations where the films were shown and the effects of the films. Local television affiliates were encouraged to develop educational programs to go along with the films, and these varied in intensity.

Warnings of Possible Contagion

Just before "Surviving" (the fourth film mentioned) was shown on network television, warnings were issued by the American Psychiatric Association, the American Academy of Pediatrics, and the American Academy of Child Psychiatry that parents should not allow their children to watch the film alone, but should join in the viewing and encourage questions and discussion. These caveats appeared in many newspapers in both the United States and Canada. Dr. Joseph Sanders of the American Academy of Pediatrics Committee on Adolescence (cited in McCormack, 1985), suggested that if a youngster was depressed over a broken love affair or any other situation, there might be something in the film to cause him to become suicidal.

In "Surviving," two teenagers commit suicide by sitting inside a car left running in a closed garage. Eleven days after the the broadcast, a teenager died in his car of carbon monoxide poisoning. The father of the boy blamed the movie for his son's death.

Imitation of Suicide in Other Media Presentations

The motion picture, "An Officer and a Gentleman," in which a young man hanged himself, was cited in a number of news reports as the apparent trigger event for an imitative pattern of suicide over a 3-month period in Westchester, New York. In another incident, which was considered to be a case of accidental death because of the age of the victim, a 6-year-old hanged himself after watching a cartoon in which a character was hanged. The parents of the child sued the cartoon syndicate and collected an undisclosed sum under the condition that they would not reveal the amount of the settlement.

Although no deaths have been attributed specifically to the cartoon in question, the members of the BADD organization have voiced considerable concern regarding the presentation of "Dungeons and Dragons" as a cartoon (Pulling, personal communication, 1987).

POSSIBLE EXPLANATIONS OF THE IMITATIVE EFFECTS OF SUICIDE

Witnessing the pain that a suicide has brought to friends, family, and other adults (including school personnel) undoubtedly contributes to the child's understanding that this is a way of inflicting punishment on others. Further, movies, films, and "docudramas" may give young people the impression that they can become celebrities by committing suicide.

Providing information to young people about the contagious effects of suicide may create additional problems. Students who have watched films or read reports about suicides have verbalized the fear that they might kill themselves without meaning to do so.

SUICIDE CLUSTERS

No facet of the youth suicide problem is more discussed than the phenomenon of suicide clusters (Coleman, 1986). The numbers of cluster suicides have increased in recent years (American Psychiatric Association, 1985), which has become a source of great concern among parents, educators, mental health workers, and public officials in the North American continent.

Rosenberg (cited in Coleman, 1986) has defined a suicide cluster as a group of suicides that are closely associated in time and space, generally a series of more than three deaths. Clusters are apparently triggered by imitation of one or more suicides within a group, a school, or a community.

> Suicide clusters appear to demonstrate the Werther effect—one teen suicide suggests another, and so on, within a community. But the news media's attention to the phenomenon appears to be part of the "reflective factor"—that is, that although the phenomenon, we speculate, may exist, in varying degrees throughout the country, it is only when a prominent story gains national status are other possible clusters publicized. (Coleman, 1986, p. 6)

Coleman (1986, 1987) has conducted an extensive review of both historical and current suicide clusters, particularly among young people. He has included detailed accounts of clusters in Plano and Clear Lake, Texas; Westchester, Rockland, and Putnam Counties, New York; Leominster and Spencer, Massachusetts; Manitoulin Island, Ontario; Omaha, Nebraska; and Mankato, Minnesota. Coleman has also noted that the incidence of suicide clusters appears to be increasing, and that they are only the latest "manifestation of the pressures of our times" (1987, p. 49).

What are the causes of cluster suicides? The causes of cluster suicides among young people are still unknown. It may be that the children kill themselves in an effort to gain the same outpouring of attention, sympathy, and grief that followed the earlier suicide. Perhaps the suicide of one young person prompts others with similar problems or in similar circumstances to follow suit. It may be that just knowing about a suicide causes a youngster to think that suicide is an option, that it is expected, that it is appropriate, or that he is assisting in "making a statement." It may also be that some of the children do not understand the permanence of death. This phenomenon may also be media related, in that many famous actors have "died" many times on the screen and are obviously still alive (Guetzloe, 1987).

Publicizing Suicides

Many authorities now believe that publicizing suicide leads to more deaths among young people, particularly among impressionable adolescents who know each other, have similar reasons for wanting to die, or feel guilty about the death of a friend. In many clusters, most of the victims lived in the same region, were of approximately the same ages, and used similar methods, such as in the widely publicized clusters in New York, on the Wind River Indian reservation in Wyoming, and in Bergenfield, New Jersey. In other instances, the cluster suicides have been committed by people of different ages, using disparate methods, and who apparently had different reasons for wanting to die.

Bergenfield Suicides

The most highly publicized suicides in the last several years were those of four young people in Bergenfield, New Jersey, who killed themselves by carbon monoxide poisoning in an apartment garage on March 11, 1987. The news of this tragedy was broadcast on national television networks and reported on the front pages of newspapers across the continent, in precisely the manner, as discussed above, that had been previously found to precipitate other suicides and attempts (Gould, M. S., & Shaffer, 1986; Phillips & Carstensen, 1986). Commentators on television news programs even noted that they were aware of the danger of contagion, but that they thought the public had a right to the information.

As expected by those who have studied youth suicide, the copycat pattern of suicide began. Within a week, there were nine other suicides and several attempts reported across the country, most of which were by carbon monoxide poisoning. Two of the attempts were in the same garage in which the four youngsters in Bergenfield had died, a vivid exemplification of the copycat phenomenon (Podhoretz, 1987).

CONTAGION RELATED TO SUICIDE ATTEMPTS

In addition to the contagious effects of completed suicide, there is evidence of imitation among young people who have attempted suicide. They are more likely than nonsuicidal patients to know or to be close to others who have shown suicidal behavior or talked about suicidal thoughts (Kreitman et al., 1970; Tishler & McKenry, 1982).

CONTAGION IN PSYCHIATRIC INSTITUTIONS

Hawton (1978, 1986) has discussed the epidemic nature of self-destructive behavior among young people in psychiatric institutions. He suggested several reasons for this—that there is generally a high concentration of suicidal patients in such institutions; that patients are usually hospitalized because they are facing severe stresses; that suicidal behavior usually attracts increased attention from the staff, which leads to competition for such attention; and that adolescents have a tendency toward bravado, which may add to the element of competition. These explanations may have implications for school programs as well, particularly for special education programs for behaviorally disordered youth.

10. Treatment of Suicidal Youth

Despite the critical importance of the treatment process, the literature on youth suicide provides relatively little information on this topic (Motto, 1985; Otto, 1972; Seiden, 1969). Pfeffer (1986) has noted that methods of treatment for childhood suicidal behavior are the least understood and least studied aspects of this phenomenon, primarily because of the lack of (a) appropriate research instruments and (b) methods for measuring treatment effects.

According to Motto (1985), there are few special techniques for treating suicidal young people. Whether the approach is psychological, social, or pharmacological, the guidelines are the same as those for working with other disturbed youth; but the situation is more critical and the crises are more extreme. Motto has also noted that the danger of suicide can actually be increased by the stresses of therapy—a concern unique to the treatment of suicidal individuals.

EMERGENCY INTERVENTION AND ASSESSMENT

Because most suicidal behavior constitutes a crisis, emergency intervention is usually the first step in treatment. The primary goal of crisis intervention is simply to keep the youngster alive—to protect the child from life-threatening behavior or to provide life-supporting emergency medical care. (Procedures for crisis intervention in the school are discussed in Part II of this text.)

The second step in intervention is to begin a comprehensive assessment (which should be conducted by a team of professionals, including a psychiatrist, psychiatric social worker, or other trained mental health professional) that will lead to a treatment plan. One of the primary goals of the assessment process is to determine how to protect the child from further suicidal behavior while the treatment plan is implemented.

CLINICAL EVALUATION OF RISK FACTORS

Mack and Hickler (1981) have compiled a comprehensive list of factors that may increase a young person's sense of worthlessness or helplessness and that may increase the risk of suicidal behavior. According to these authors, the following factors should be carefully evaluated by a clinician in determining the possibility of suicidal tendencies:

1. The setting—the family, its place in the community, relationships in the neighborhood or town, adaptation to the values of the population.
2. The personalities of parents, principal caretakers, siblings, and other important relatives (especially with regard to child-rearing and interaction with this child).
3. Genetic and constitutional factors that might contribute to vulnerability.
4. Developmental experience, especially disturbances in early parent-child relationships.
5. Experiences of loss in childhood.
6. Emerging personality organization, especially idealized expectations for self and others.
7. Tendency toward reacting to losses or hurts with lowered self-esteem, depression, or withdrawal.
8. Recent experiences of success or failure, especially in human relationships—friendship, alienation, love, and loss.
9. Evidence of preoccupation with death, especially its emergence as a possible solution.
10. Lack of protection within the family, community, or nation "especially as experienced through television; exposure to sexual assault; expectations for performance or experiences of exploitation" (p. 194) that may lead to self-devaluation.
11. Increased acceptability of suicide as a solution.
12. Recent losses, separations, disrupted relationships, disappointments, family moves, unsuccessful treatment, appeals for help, lack of interventions.

SELF-REPORTING BY CHILDREN AND ADOLESCENTS

Several researchers have furnished evidence that children and adolescents are reliable reporters of their own symptoms of depression or suicidal behavior (Pfeffer, 1985; Puig-Antich, 1980; Robbins & Alessi, 1985). Evaluation of suicidal risk can therefore be accomplished not only by observation of warning signs but also by simply asking young people directly about their feelings and actions.

Robbins and Alessi further noted that, while an adolescent may either minimize or exaggerate symptoms in the presence of family members, these distortions seem to be minimal when the youngster is interviewed alone. These findings suggest that young people should be interviewed separately from family members during an assessment of suicidal risk.

QUESTIONS, CHECKLISTS, OR PROTOCOLS

Several authorities have suggested questions, checklists, or protocols to be used by a clinician in the assessment of potential for suicide. Some of these, which are intended for use only by psychiatrists and other highly skilled mental health professionals, are discussed here.

Corder-Haizlip Child Suicide Checklist

Corder and Haizlip (1983) have developed a checklist that may be used by mental health professionals to screen potentially suicidal children more accurately before psychiatric assessment takes place. The checklist includes questions to be addressed to the child as well as those to be addressed to parents or guardians. Versions of the checklist have appeared in an article by Corder and Haizlip (1983) and in a text by Pfeffer (1986). Although the checklist has not been standardized, Pfeffer (1986) has hailed it as an advance in the assessment of suicidal risk in children.

Questions for Evaluating Suicidal Risk in Young Children

Pfeffer (1986) has listed a variety of questions that should be asked during a psychiatric evaluation of suicidal risk in young children. These questions are grouped according to the following key areas:

1. Suicidal fantasies or actions.
2. Concepts of the outcomes of suicidal behavior.
3. Circumstances at the time of suicidal behavior.
4. Previous experiences with suicidal behavior.
5. Motivations for suicidal behavior.
6. Concepts of and experiences related to death.
7. Symptoms of depression.
8. Family and environmental situations.

The questions are in language that any school-aged child should be able to understand. Pfeffer suggested that these questions should be helpful to clinicians in structuring an interview with a potentially suicidal child.

Child Suicide Potential Scales

Pfeffer and her associates (Pfeffer, Conte, et al., 1979, 1980; Pfeffer, Zuckerman et al., 1984) have developed a battery of scales for use as research instruments in the identification of factors associated with suicidal behavior in children. Information necessary to complete the scales is gathered during the clinical interview from the child, the parents, and other knowledgeable informants. Formal scoring procedures for the scales are presently being developed (Pfeffer, 1986).

Psychological Biopsy

McIntyre and Angle (1973, 1981) devised a structured interview and rating system, called a "psychological biopsy," for use by the emergency room physician in the evaluation of children and adolescents who have made suicide attempts or gestures. The purposes of the psychological biopsy are (a) to determine if the individual intended to die, and (b) to define the nature and severity of perturbation (disturbance or agitation).

According to McIntyre and Angle (1981), the patient should be interviewed privately and assured that the information will not be used against him. In the interim, information about the immediate attempt and the individual's past history should be obtained from the family or other rescuer, if possible. According to these authors, who are physicians, confidentiality is important to the youngster's self-esteem and should be guaranteed despite pressures from legal authorities or the parents.

The psychological biopsy includes questions in three areas of inquiry: (a) the suicide attempt or gesture; (b) family and other interactions; and (c) prior difficulties, symptoms, and perturbation. Nine areas are scored in terms of risk: circumstantial lethality, prior self-destructive behavior, depression, hostility, stress, reaction of parent or parent surrogate, loss of communication with peers or adults, lack of resources (religious ties or professional help), and parental expectations and control. The following questions are modifications of those used in the psychological biopsy as proposed by McIntyre and Angle (1981):

1. Narrative outline of the suicidal event. Tell me what happened. What was the time of day? What did you do then? Did you tell anyone? Did you think you would be found? How did they find out about it? When did you first think about doing this? Have you ever done anything like this in the past? Do you think you will do anything like it again?

2. Narrative outline of family and other interactions. Tell me about the members of your family? How old are they? Where do they live? How do you get along with them? Do you think any of them uses too much alcohol or drugs? Have any of your family or close friends ever attempted suicide? Which people can you talk to when things go wrong? If you could make some changes in your life, what would you change?

3. Prior difficulties, symptoms, and perturbation. What medical problems have you had? Have you had any problems at school? Have you ever repeated a grade? Have you dropped out of school? Have you ever been suspended or expelled? Have you had any trouble with the police? Do you use drugs? Have you had any trouble because of drugs or alcohol? Have you ever run away from home? Have you been under a doctor's care because of emotional problems? Have you had any problems with your girlfriend (or boyfriend)? Have you had any problems with your friends?

EVALUATING THE CHILD'S CONCEPT OF DEATH

According to Nilson (1981) it is particularly important for the clinician to evaluate the maintenance of unrealistic ideas about death and the continuation of magical thinking when assessing a young child's potential for self-destructive behavior. Toolan (1978) has suggested that children under the age of 10 may believe in the reversibility of death and not realize the permanence of suicidal acts. Religious beliefs should also be evaluated, because the child may see death as peaceful or may believe in reincarnation or resurrection and expect to return to this life or to another. (Additional information about the young child's concept of death may be found in Chapter 7.)

Child's Understanding of Lethality

Shneidman (1975) has defined lethality as the probability of a person's killing himself in the immediate future; the greater the probability of death, the greater the level of lethality. The determination of the level of lethality of the suicide plan is further discussed in Part II of this text.

Assessment of lethality in children is difficult because the child may not understand the lethal potential of certain actions or agents (Pfeffer, 1986). They may think, for example, that a few aspirin would cause death and a leap from a high place would not. Pfeffer has suggested, therefore, that the assessment of lethality is not as important in the evaluation of suicidal children as it is with older individuals; but any suicidal impulses in children should be regarded as serious and potentially fatal.

NEED FOR FAMILY PHYSICIANS TO NOTICE SUICIDAL BEHAVIOR

Several authorities have suggested that physicians must become more sensitive to the possibility of suicidal behavior in both adults and children. According to Shneidman and Mandelkorn (1970), fully three-fourths of all suicide victims have seen a physician within the 4 months previous to the day on which they kill themselves. The American Academy of Pediatrics (cited in Mason, 1985) has reported that 75% of adolescent suicide victims had seen a physician within 1 month of their death.

According to Pfeffer (1986), pediatricians may be unaware of both the diagnostic indicators of suicidal behavior in children and the required forms of treatment. She has suggested that there is an urgent need to educate physicians and other professionals who work with children to recognize the signs of potential suicide and to recommend psychiatric consultation for all children with suicidal ideation or behavior.

WHO SHOULD BE INVOLVED IN THE DIAGNOSTIC PROCESS?

Pfeffer (1986) has suggested that, because of the complex nature of suicidal behavior in children and the variety of potential and psychosocial interventions, highly trained and experienced specialists in child psychiatry or child mental health should be involved in the initial diagnostic evaluation and the formulation of a treatment plan. The plan may subsequently require the services of other professionals who have expertise in a particular aspect of the treatment program.

When suicidal young people require psychiatric inpatient treatment, or when they are suffering from psychiatric disorder, the involvement of psychiatrists and other highly skilled medical personnel is essential. On the other hand, Hawton & Catalan (1982) have cited evidence that treatment of suicidal individuals by social workers, nonmedical therapists, mental health workers, and volunteers may often be as effective as the more traditional forms of care by psychiatrists.

CRISIS INTERVENTION IN THE CLINICAL SETTING

Intervention with the Acutely Suicidal

Shneidman (1985) has suggested several specific measures for dealing with an acutely suicidal person, including (a) reducing psychological pain, (b) addressing frustrated needs, (c) blocking the exit (preventing the individual from committing suicide), and (d) offering viable options to suicide. He has also emphasized the necessity for hospitalizing seriously suicidal individuals.

Therapeutic strategies that Shneidman (1975) has suggested for use with the seriously suicidal include the following:

1. Continuous (daily, if possible) monitoring of the person's potential for suicide.

2. Consultation (by the psychotherapist) with other therapists, to discuss not only the treatment but also the therapist's feelings.

3. Attention to therapeutic transference (actively promoting life rather than death, showing concern, increasing the frequency of therapy sessions, giving transfusions of hope and nurturance).

4. Working directly with significant others (family, close friends).

5. Modifying the "usual canons of confidentiality" by refusing to be a partner in the patient's plans for death (Shneidman, 1975, p. 1782).

Intervention with the Chronically Suicidal

Some young people who commit suicide are chronically suicidal. Their deaths, according to Peck (1985), are the result of their pathological lifestyles rather than acute situational stress. Crisis intervention is only partially or temporarily effective in preventing the suicides of these youngsters; they require different, multiple, and more intensive interventions. Of critical importance is continued close supervision, so that suicide is not possible.

TREATMENT OPTIONS FOR SUICIDAL YOUTH

There are a number of possibilities for treatment of suicidal children and adolescents, including hospitalization, medication, short-term or long-term inpatient or outpatient therapy, or a combination of any or all of these. According to Pfeffer (1986), some of the general goals of treatment for suicidal behavior are to protect the child from harm, to decrease suicidal tendencies and vulnerability to suicidal behavior, to decrease risk factors, and to enhance factors that may protect against suicidal tendencies.

Psychiatric Hospitalization

If assessment reveals a serious risk of imminent suicide, psychiatric hospitalization is considered to be the most effective acute intervention (Pfeffer, 1978; Richman, 1981, 1986). According to Richman, hospitalization, with adequate preparation for admission and discharge and with involvement of the family in the treatment program, can be very effective as well as lifesaving at the time. The decision to hospitalize a suicidal child or adolescent is usually based on one or more of the following factors:

1. The young person has made a serious suicide attempt or is threatening to do so.
2. The child's suicidal state is associated with signs of either serious psychiatric disorder (particularly depression or schizophrenia) or drug addiction.
3. The family cannot provide adequate supervision or support.
4. The family appear to be indifferent, angry, or rejecting (Eisenberg, 1980; Richman, 1986).

Reaction to Therapy As a Factor. An additional factor in making the decision to hospitalize is the negative reaction of the youngster to outpatient therapy and treatment. According to Litman (1970), if a suicidal patient does not form an alliance with the therapist during the first few hours of outpatient therapy, the hazards of this treatment mode are greatly increased, and hospitalization should be considered.

Factors to be Considered with Young Children. Pfeffer and Plutchik (1982), in a study of 103 psychiatric patients, ages 6 to 12 years, identified variables related to the need for hospital placement. According to Pfeffer (1986), the level of severity of the following should be considered in making a decision regarding hospitalization of a young child: (a) the degree of the child's assaultive behavior, (b) the seriousness of suicidal behavior, (c) antisocial behavior, (d) poor reality testing, (e) complications during the mother's pregnancy with the child, and (f) separation of the parents.

Inpatient Treatment of Suicidal Youth. The specific treatment available in a psychiatric hospital depends to a great degree on the orientation of the administrators and staff, but there are certain procedures that are applicable in most hospital settings. The primary purposes of hospitalization are (a) to protect the child from suicidal behavior; (b) to remove him from environmental stresses; (c) to decrease isolation by providing frequent, prolonged, and therapeutic human contact; (d) to reduce distress; (e) to conduct a comprehensive assessment; and (f) to plan, implement, and evaluate the treatment program (Pfeffer, 1986). The treatment plan may call for medication, and, particularly with young people, there is a need to monitor the effects while dosage and diet can be controlled. To the fullest extent feasible, children and adolescents (as well as adults) should be informed of the reasons for hospitalization, their goals, and their progress.

Benefits of Hospitalization. In addition to protection from harm, there are several other important advantages in psychiatric hospitalization of suicidal youth. The hospital is a self-contained setting in which the therapeutic efforts of many professionals can be coordinated. The child can be observed in a variety of individual and group activities—school, eating, sleeping, recreation, therapy, and informal interaction with peers and adults. Any physical problems can be evaluated and treated. Further, as discussed above, treatment can be both controlled and monitored.

Problems with Hospitalization. There has been considerable recent criticism of hospital treatment of disturbed youth. Newspaper and television reports have pointed to the increased use of psychiatric hospitalization for children and adolescents for whom such treatment was either ineffective or contraindicated. Psychiatrists have agreed that the young patient's insurance coverage may be a primary consideration. Further, as discussed by Richman (1986), there is some evidence that hospital treatment of suicidal individuals may be ineffective. The suicide rate among hospitalized patients is among the highest of any group, with the highest risk associated with the period around admission to or discharge from a mental hospital. Some suicides are even precipitated by hospitalization or the threat of hospitalization.

Richman (1986) has discussed other major criticisms regarding hospitalization of the suicidal individual, including the following:

1. It may eliminate the family from participating in the treatment program.
2. It creates a disruption between the patient and his social functioning.
3. It may furnish an undesirable model for future crises, leading to repeated hospitalizations rather than fostering a self-help or problem-solving attitude in the patient and the family.
4. It may be perceived by the family to be an indication that the patient is incurable and "will end up in the back wards of a Bedlam or snakepit" (p. 84).

Family Therapy

Family counseling or therapy is generally regarded as the approach of choice for suicidal individuals, regardless of age, but particularly for children and young adolescents who will be remaining in the family (Brown, 1985; Richman, 1981, 1986). According to Richman (1986), the advantages of family therapy include the following:

1. It is particularly suited to keeping troubled individuals in the community, which is the new goal of psychiatry.
2. It can be combined with medication and other biological treatment modalities as well as with both individual and group therapy.
3. It can be used in a wide variety of settings—hospital, clinic, private office, or home (Richman, 1986).

Family Therapy for Young Children. Suicidal behavior of young children, according to Pfeffer (1981), must always be considered a family problem; therefore, family therapy is usually the treatment of choice. The decision for outpatient family therapy, however, depends to a great extent upon the psychosocial resources of the family, which must be carefully evaluated (Eisenberg, 1980).

If the parents show understanding and concern, counseling on an outpatient basis is feasible. On the other hand, if the parents are indifferent—and worse, if they are angry, show no understanding of the stress presented by the attempt, and cannot be supportive—then hospitalization will be necessary. Failure of the gesture to bring about an affirmation of genuine concern may serve to confirm the patient's worse fears of being unloved; the parent who belittles the youngster as a failure may make it necessary for the youngster to try again to preserve face (Eisenberg, 1980, p. 319).

Goals of Family Therapy. Eisenberg (1980) has emphasized the importance of rebuilding hope and reestablishing healthy ties among family members. "Because the patient feels unloved and unworthy of love, the task of treatment is to convey a sense of caring and to restore faith in the possibility of a satisfying future . . . to restore to the patient the sources of emotional sustenance which all of us depend on for our survival" (p. 319). Another goal of family therapy is to assist parents in modifying their perceptions of the child, particularly with respect to aggressive feelings or death wishes (Ackerly, 1967).

Pfeffer (1986) has listed several goals for family therapy with suicidal children that include the following: (a) to help parents to understand the seriousness of the child's suicidal tendencies and the need for effective interventions, (b) to define and remediate marital conflicts that interfere with parenting responsibilities, (c) to reduce the parents' inappropriate behaviors, and (d) to treat any severe parental psychiatric disturbances. Pfeffer has further suggested that all family members—siblings, grandparents, aunts, and cousins—who are intimately involved with the child should also be involved in the initial evaluation and treatment planning.

Short-Term Therapies

Among the newer forms of therapy are several that are considered to be short term in nature. Short-term therapies have proved to be successful with suicidal adults, but only a few have been evaluated in terms of their usefulness with children or adolescents (Hawton, 1986).

Cognitive Therapy. Cohen-Sandler et al. (1982) developed a cognitive approach to train suicidal children to solve problems in nonsuicidal ways. The problem-solving training program took place in seven 45-minute individual sessions on consecutive days. The therapists used presentations, visual materials, modeling, role playing, and discussions to teach social and empathy skills and cognitive problem solving. The treatment was found to increase the suicidal children's forethought, social knowledge, appreciation for the consequences of behavior, and the ability to generate more solutions to conflicts.

Group Problem-Solving Therapy. Wallach and Nilson (cited in Nilson, 1981) have developed a short-term group problem-solving therapy, primarily for a runaway and delinquent population, that may also be useful with suicidal youngsters. The approach, which makes extensive use of role playing, was effective in improving the youngsters' problem-solving skills. Nilson (1981) has pointed out, however, that longer term individual therapy, preferably with family involvement, may be necessary for completely effective intervention.

Brief Problem-Oriented Treatment. Hawton and Catalan (1982) have developed a brief problem-oriented approach for treating self-poisoners that focuses on helping the patients to solve their own problems. The principles of this problem-solving approach are as follows:

1. Define the problems to be tackled, dividing the problems into two types—those requiring a choice between alternatives and those requiring the attainment of specific objectives.
2. Establish realistic and specific goals.
3. Clarify the steps necessary to achieve the goals and the possible consequences.
4. Agree on tasks to be accomplished before the next session.

At the next session, the therapist and the patient review the patient's progress in carrying out the tasks. The therapist offers praise and encouragement for any progress made, and subsequent tasks are selected. If the patient has failed to accomplish the previously chosen task, the therapist and the patient explore the possible reasons. The therapist should help the patient to recognize actions or attitudes that might have kept him from achieving his objectives. If the task was inappropriate or too demanding, alternative approaches should be explored, or the task could be broken down into more manageable steps (Hawton & Catalan, 1982).

Other components of this treatment approach include modification of attitudes, facilitation of communication, contracting, providing information, offering advice, referral to other agencies, setting limits to treatment, and preparing the patient for future crises (preventive measures).

Indications for Short-Term Therapy. Pfeffer (1986) has noted that long-term psychotherapy is indicated for most suicidal children. She has cited the following example, however, of a situation for which short-term therapy may be indicated:

A child with a learning disability who is transferred to a new school that does not have a remedial program suited to the child's specific needs may feel so stressed that the child entertains suicidal ideation. Brief psychotherapy in conjunction with special educational assistance may decrease the school stress and increase the child's sense of self-worth and confidence. (Pfeffer, 1986, pp. 221-222)

Need for Both Short-Term and Long-Term Therapy

According to many therapists, most suicidal youth need both crisis-oriented (short-term) and intensive (long-term) therapy of either group or individual nature (Brown, 1985; Rosenkrantz, 1978; Toolan, 1978). The suicidal situation is most frequently a crisis, but the underlying problems will require long-term treatment.

PROBLEMS IN THERAPY WITH SUICIDAL YOUTH

Many therapists have noted that working with any suicidal individual is extremely difficult, even for a highly trained and skilled professional. Richman (1986) has referred to the treatment of a suicidal person as a "profound and shaking experience" (p. 67). For a variety of reasons, working with suicidal youth is often even more difficult.

Parental Resistance to Treatment

Mental health professionals have often cited parental resistance to treatment as a problem in working with suicidal youth (Hawton, 1986; Morrison & Collier, 1969; Motto, 1985; Richman, 1986). Morrison and Collier (1969) found that, of 30 families referred for therapy because of suicide attempts by children and adolescents, only 8 continued after the initial interview, and most of those families terminated treatment (against the judgment of the therapist) after three or four sessions.

Resistance of Young People to Therapy

Motto (1985) has found that young people themselves are often resistant to entering therapy. He has cited the example of college students who fear that they would be considered unfit for an academic or professional career if they seek assistance for emotional problems. As previously noted, suicidal teenagers also refuse to seek assistance for emotional problems because they do not want to be considered mentally ill (Blumenthal, 1985).

Motto (1985) has also suggested that a young person who is markedly depressed may not be able to handle the demands of insight therapy or intensive exploration. The concerned attention of a therapist may be very threatening to young people who are ambivalent about dependency and who must disrupt any developing relationship or sense of intimacy (Motto, 1985). Mack and Hickler (1981) have also observed that adolescents are not the best candidates for therapy, primarily because they tend to see adult counselors as "official parent representatives" (p. 224).

TREATMENT WITH MEDICATION

According to Richman (1986), medication is the most frequent form of aftercare treatment for suicidal individuals, but it should not be considered sufficient by itself. Further, the use of medication with children and adolescents is still extremely controversial. Gadow (1986) has provided a comprehensive discussion of pharmocological treatment of children, which should be useful to teachers in understanding the effects of the various types of medication prescribed for depressed or suicidal students.

Medication of Adolescents

Frederick (1985) has discussed some of the problems in the use of medication with adolescents. He has noted that antidepressant drugs can be useful, but they may not take effect for several weeks, and, in the meantime, a life could be lost. Sedating or tranquilizing suicidal youngsters may reduce anxiety, but the underlying problems have not been solved.

Many physicians are concerned about the possibility of drug overdose if the suicidal youngster is not hospitalized or properly supervised. This concern is not without basis. There have been many reports of deaths due to deliberate or accidental overdose of legal medications.

According to Frederick (1985), tricyclic antidepressants are preferred to monoamine oxidase inhibitors for use with adolescents because there are fewer serious side effects associated with tricyclics. Serious side effects may occur, however, when certain foods are mixed with monoamine oxidase inhibitors. Among the problem foods are those that contain tyramine, which is found in proteins dependent on the aging process (e.g., sausage, sour cream herring, red wine, dried fish, avocados, and chicken liver). Frederick has further noted that the use of antidepressant medication is more suitable for older adolescents whose body weights are equivalent to those of adults.

Medication of Young Children

Cohen-Sandler et al. (1982) found that medication was rarely used by pediatricians in the treatment of depressed children. When pharmacological treatment was indicated, the drugs of choice were antidepressants. Pfeffer (1986), who has reviewed a number of studies related to the use of medication with suicidal children, has suggested that the antidepressant imipramine is a valuable adjunct to treatment of severely depressed suicidal children.

Combination Approach

According to Frederick (1985), a combination of therapeutic approaches should be used with a suicidal youngster. Tranquilizers or sedatives should be used at the onset if the individual is in an acute state, followed by verbal crisis intervention and psychotherapy.

NEED FOR CONSTANT SUPERVISION OF SUICIDAL YOUTH

The need for supervision is one of the most critical issues related to treatment of suicidal youth. If the suicidal youngster is in outpatient therapy, the family must ensure that weapons and prescription drugs are destroyed, discarded, or otherwise made unavailable. In the hospital as well, patients should be under constant supervision, so that makeshift weapons and means are not available. Even in a psychiatric hospital, there is no assurance that a suicide will not occur.

A 15-year-old male escaped from the psychiatric ward of a large hospital and fled in a van that he stole from the hospital parking lot. A few blocks from the hospital, he crashed into the vehicle in front of him, leaped from the van, and threw himself under the wheels of a passing truck.

The boy lived, but suffered massive head injuries and is now severely retarded. He had been hospitalized for suicidal behavior, having previously attempted suicide in the same manner.

A SUPPORTIVE NETWORK AS AN ADJUNCT TO TREATMENT

Many authorities have suggested the creation of a support group for a suicidal child—a network of individuals who interact with the youngster during daily activities and who can help carry out the treatment program. The group would include school personnel, peers, and other individuals important to the child. According to Pfeffer (1986), these individuals should have direct access to both the therapist, who can give advice regarding interventions and interactions with the child, and the parents, with whom they would discuss the child's progress. Assessment of the strengths and weaknesses of a young person's supportive network is an important facet of planning for an appropriate treatment program.

11. A Shared Responsibility

Why should suicide prevention be a function of the school? Aside from the legal requirements in districts in which prevention programs have been mandated, the school has certain moral and ethical responsibilities to protect and nurture the children who are entrusted to its care. Clarizio and McCoy (1983) have noted that the school has access to large numbers of children and youth over long periods of time during the formative years, and that it also has "a culturally sanctioned right to 'interfere' in other people's business, at least to the extent that the interference pertains to the child's educability" (p. 641).

SCHOOL AS A SOURCE OF EDUCATION AND TRAINING

There is little argument that the school should be the pivotal institution for providing educational interventions—especially those aimed at helping young people. The school has already accepted the responsibility for providing information—to both children and adults—regarding a host of societal problems. There is still considerable controversy, however, regarding the type and extent of the suicide prevention programs that should be offered in the school. The problem of possible contagion is discussed in Chapter 9. Suggestions regarding instructional materials and methods of presentation are included in Chapter 20.

SCHOOL AS A SOURCE OF "RESCUERS"

Children are much more likely to come into contact with potential rescuers in the school than they are in other community settings. This is especially true for younger children, who cannot move freely in the community. In many instances, the child's problems, particularly those related to academics or the peer group, are more evident in the school setting than they are in the home, and teachers and other educational personnel are now trained to recognize the signs of distress and provide appropriate interventions. Further, the character-istic problems of a broken home or dysfunctional family, while not necessarily a direct cause of suicidal behavior, reduce the possibility of rescue in that setting.

TO WHAT EXTENT SHOULD THE SCHOOL BE INVOLVED?

Many authorities have recognized the importance of the school in providing a comprehensive program of suicide prevention for children and adolescents (Berkovitz, 1985; Havighurst, 1969; Jacobs, 1971; Mack & Hickler, 1981; Pfeffer, 1986; Ross, 1985).

Researchers at CDC have recommended that schools and communi-ties develop cooperative plans that include not only a system for early detection and referral of depressed or suicidal students, but also steps to be taken to avoid panic in the event of a completed suicide (Strother, 1986). These activities, often suggested by suicide prevention experts, are the major thrusts of most of the school-based programs that have already been established across the continent.

Providing a Positive Environment

A comprehensive program of primary prevention would provide for a positive and supportive environment. Among the components of such a positive environment are humane laws; reasonable rules; provision of basic needs—food, shelter, and clothing; physical safety and comfort; psychological security; avoidance of punishment; opportunities for socialization; attainable goals; success experiences; and adults who are appropriate models of self-control and self-esteem. The provision of these components in the home, school, and community would obviously be difficult, but not impossible. An important consideration for educators is the determination of the extent to which the school should accept the responsibility for meeting the basic needs of its students.

Educators generally agree that schools must provide support and assistance to students in time of trouble (Luty, 1985). Mental health professionals have suggested that the schools assume even greater responsibilities in providing for the emotional well being of children and youth. Stickney (1968) has suggested that schools should become more like mental health centers; Ross (1980) has advocated for special programs for depressed and suicidal students; and Berkovitz (1985) has suggested that schools should become more relevant by addressing the developmental tasks of students.

According to Berkovitz (1985), there are several elements that schools must provide if they are to contribute effectively to the prevention of youth suicide: (a) a general positive mental health atmosphere in the individual school or district; (b) an optimum level of psychological services; and (c) plans for prevention, intervention, and postvention. He has further suggested the establishment (within the school) of a helping network of students, facilitated by either a group counseling program or by the presence of involved school personnel.

The rules, procedures, and curricula within the school or district should be examined in the light of whether they contribute to the emotional health of the students. To ensure a positive school environment, changes may be necessary in district policies or procedures related to grading, promotion, testing, placement, graduation, discipline, or selection and retention of teachers and administrators.

COMMUNITY RESPONSIBILITY IN SUICIDE PREVENTION

Community cooperation and support are essential in providing an effective suicide prevention program; the school alone cannot accept this charge. It may even be that youth suicide will never be preventable without major societal changes that are beyond the purview of any one community, state, province, or nation.

According to Hawton (1986), measures that would help to prevent youth suicide include the following, some of which are obviously the responsibility of the community (or society) rather than the school:

1. Social support for dysfunctional families.
2. Improvement in diagnosis and treatment of depression and other psychiatric disorders.
3. Educational programs in child and adolescent psychology for the medical community.
4. Training in the problems of childhood and adolescence for parents, school personnel, and mental health professionals.

Eisenberg (1984), basing his suggestions on a summary of recent research findings, has proposed several specific thrusts for the prevention of youth suicide, including (a) early detection of depression or suicidal behavior, (b) limiting access to lethal weapons, and (c) limiting publicity associated with suicide. Although the school can provide assistance in the early detection of suicidal behavior, it can have very little effect upon limiting either publicity or access to weapons.

RESPONSIBILITIES OF GOVERNMENTAL SERVICES AND AGENCIES

A review of the risk factors related to youth suicide reveals several specific areas of concern that fall under the jurisdiction of local, state, province, or national agencies and organizations. Depression and suicidal behavior have been found to be related to numerous other problems encountered by children in the home, school, and community. To assure that children at risk for suicide do not "fall between the cracks," the following provisions, the responsibilities of various governmental agencies, are essential:

1. Improved and expanded services for handicapped children, runaways, juvenile offenders, drug abusers, school dropouts, children in need of medical services, neglected children, children from single-parent families, pregnant adolescents, and children who have been physically, sexually, or psychologically abused, all of whom are at risk for suicidal behavior.
2. Programs that provide for early detection of suicidal behavior in community facilities such as hospitals, clinics, day care centers, recreation programs, supervised playgrounds, group homes, and shelters, where children gather or are placed by parents, guardians, or agencies.
3. Changes in rules, regulations, policies, and procedures in juvenile courts, detention centers, and other facilities in which young people are incarcerated, to provide for early detection of suicidal behavior, crisis intervention, psychiatric assessment, medical care, counseling or therapy, education, vocational training, and humane treatment.

These suggestions are further discussed in the following sections.

Improved and Expanded Services for Children at Risk

The provision of basic needs for children at risk is a moral, ethical, and political issue. There is a critical need, in the United States and Canada, as well as other countries around the world, for more and better services for children. Professional organizations, parent groups, community leaders, and other influential individuals must bring pressure to bear on those who can effect the changes. Governmental leaders, who are in a position to ensure support for children in need, must accept their responsibility in this regard. If the support systems continue to crumble, the children will not survive.

Early Detection of Suicidal Behavior in Other Settings

As previously discussed, many authorities have recognized the importance of the early detection of signs of depression and suicidal behavior, and the schools have accepted their share of this responsibility. Children and adolescents, however, also function in several other arenas—in the home, in day care, in the peer group outside the school, in churches, in organizations, in sports programs, in recreational facilities, in jobs, and in community facilities. They are attended by a variety of adults—day care workers, physicians, dentists, nurses, neighbors, coaches, youth counselors, ministers, law enforcement agents, employers, supervisors, and co-workers. Each of these individuals and institutions should also assume responsibility for the detection and referral of children in need of assistance. Information about the symptoms of depression or suicidal tendencies should be included in the training programs for all individuals— professionals and volunteers alike—who come in contact with children and youth.

Changes in Laws and Policies

There is an urgent need for changes in the laws and policies that specifically affect children and adolescents, such as those governing divorce, separation, custody, placement, abuse, neglect, and supervision. Of particular importance are laws related to arrest, detention, and incarceration of young people.

In a study prepared for the Office of Juvenile Justice and Delinquency Prevention, it was estimated that approximately 479,000 children were confined in adult jails and lockups in the United States in 1978 (Charle, 1981). There have been numerous reports of the suicides of young people who have been incarcerated for minor offenses. Many of these children were jailed for status offenses— offenses that are crimes only because the individual involved is not an adult. Incarceration for a status offense is a waste of governmental funds and sometimes a waste of a young person's life.

A 16-year-old boy was arrested and taken to a juvenile detention center. A few hours after his arrest, he tied a bedsheet to the bars of his cell and hanged himself. He had been arrested for truancy.

Screening, Diagnosis, and Treatment Programs. There is also a tremendous need for programs in jails and other detention facilities that provide for screening for suicidal behavior as well as diagnosis and treatment of depression or other psychiatric disorders. Screening and surveillance are particularly important in the first few hours after a youngster is arrested, as evidenced by the case mentioned above. According to a study by the Michigan Department of Corrections, the majority of jail suicides are committed in the first 24 hours after arrest, and many during the first 12 hours (Charle, 1981). Further, prompt disposition of minor offense cases, rather than lengthy periods of incarceration, would also save lives.

A teenager hanged himself in jail. He had been imprisoned for over 2 weeks after being arrested for a minor offense. He had been unable to post bond.

Special Treatment for Troubled Youth. Screening, diagnostic, and treatment programs would also provide guidance for making decisions regarding the seriousness of an offense and the probabilities of a prisoner's harming others. Moving the prisoner who would not be dangerous into a less restrictive setting might save a life. The following is an example of correctional overkill.

An 18-year-old hanged himself in his jail cell. He had been accused of making a verbal threat to kill the President during an obscene telephone call to a woman. According to police investigators, the young man had made no attempt to actually reach the President. He had been in jail for 5 months.

It should be noted that the young person in this case would be considered, in most instances, to be an adult. It is unfortunate that criminal law and laws affecting civil rights do not work together for the protection of young people who may be suffering from handicapping emotional problems. Our nations have laws that provide for education for the handicapped; they do not provide for humane treatment.

Question of Security. A problem that is particularly troubling is that young people are in danger of being beaten, raped, or murdered in detention facilities. As feared by the youngster who killed himself because he was afraid that he would be raped in jail (a case included in the discussion on risk factors in this text), incarceration brings more risks than just the loss of freedom, opportunity, and self-respect. It is unconscionable that prisoners are not guaranteed physical safety. The system that prevents their escape from the facility has made it impossible for them to escape from one another.

LIMITING ACCESS TO WEAPONS

Eisenberg (1986) has pointed out that the impulse to commit suicide, especially in a young person, commonly waxes and wanes and that suicidal actions often depend on the availability of a selected means. Some methods are not acceptable to certain individuals, even if they have strong intentions to kill themselves. When highly lethal methods are not available, young people do not necessarily choose other means. Further, the fact that an individual can be temporarily deterred from commiting a suicidal act increases the chances for rescue (Frederick, 1985). "If opportunity and means for suicide are not at hand, young persons survive the critical period and their spirits usually spring back" (Eisenberg, 1986, p. 706).

Although such lethal means as tall buildings, traffic, articles of clothing, razors, ropes, and bodies of water may often be readily available, the community and the home should cooperate to reduce the accessibility of guns and medication. Firearms and poisoning (usually with legal drugs) are the two most common methods of suicide among the young (Cantor, 1985).

Limiting Firearm Accessibility

Firearms and explosives (generally firearms) account for by far the greatest number of suicidal deaths in the United States each year in all age groups (CDC, 1985, 1986). According to Cantor (1985), 65% of all teen suicides are committed with guns. There is no doubt that the ready availability of firearms makes violent acts, such as suicide, easier to commit; there is no more lethal method.

Parents must assume the primary responsibility for keeping firearms out of the hands of children who live at home, but the community at large should be responsible for promoting laws and programs that limit the opportunities for children and adolescents to avail themselves of this most lethal means. Parents, educators, law enforcement officials, and lawmakers must be made aware of their individual responsibilities in this regard.

A program that involves the cooperation of police and parents to reduce young people's access to firearms has been developed by the Handgun Information Center (1984). The Center has published a brochure that emphasizes practical suggestions for adults regarding the storage, maintenance, and handling of handguns as well as appropriate training for their use. The brochure also stresses the importance of keeping guns out of the hands of children, criminals, and individuals who are either mentally ill or under the influence of alcohol or drugs.

Limiting Access to Lethal Drugs

Poisoning, usually with prescription medication, is the second most common method of suicide, accounting for approximately 11% of all suicides, and is the most common method used in attempts by young females (Cantor, 1985). Access to lethal drugs could be reduced by limiting the number of pills in each prescription. Parents could also simply keep prescription drugs in locked storage. Young people who are taking antidepressant medication should do so under supervision, so that pills cannot be hoarded. Further, when potentially lethal drugs are being used, an antidote, which could be administered in case of either accidental or intentional overdose, should also be made available to the patient. Physicians and pharmacists should also accept the responsibility for informing patients about the possible lethality of their medications and the need for appropriate storage.

LIMITING PUBLICITY ABOUT SUICIDE

Eisenberg (1986), in a discussion of the effects of media events upon suicide rates among the young, has suggested the following:

> In view of the importance of the public health problem, the strength of the evidence for the phenomenon of imitative suicide, and the need to formulate public policy even while additional studies are being undertaken, it is timely to ask whether there are measures that should be taken to limit media coverage of suicide. (p. 706)

Need for an Informed Public

Eisenberg (1986) has acknowledged that the public lacks the moral or civil authority to manipulate the media. Such interference would violate the norms for a free press and an informed public.

Need for Self-Regulation

As discussed in the section on contagion, several recent studies have shown that both news releases and fictional accounts of suicide are associated with temporary increases in the suicide rates, particularly among teenagers. The evidence is too strong for the public (and the media) to ignore. Representatives from the media should develop self-regulatory guidelines for the reporting of suicides—especially those of children and adolescents. Merely printing the reports in the middle of a section rather than on the front page of the newspaper might prove to be life saving.

COMMUNITY PARTICIPATION IN THE SCHOOL'S SUICIDE PREVENTION PROGRAM

The cooperation of community agencies, mental health professionals, and lay persons is vital to the success of a school suicide prevention program. As discussed in Part II of this text, the planning committee should include community leaders, representatives from community organizations, legislators, and other officials, who can provide valuable assistance in determining needs and procuring additional resources.

Schools and community mental health professionals must also cooperate in providing crisis intervention, treatment, and support for suicidal students. The school should not attempt to duplicate services that are readily available in the community. Suicide prevention, along with other health and social services, should be a total community effort; saving lives is everybody's business.

12. Public Health Model: Three Levels of Prevention

According to the public health model, prevention activity may be classified as occurring at the primary, secondary, or tertiary level, depending on the stage in the disease process at which the activity is implemented. The purpose of primary prevention is to lower the incidence of certain problems in the population, to keep problems from occurring. Secondary prevention involves the early identification of those who have symptoms of disease or disorder and the provision of therapeutic intervention, thereby preventing more serious problems. Tertiary prevention is the treatment of those who are already seriously or chronically ill. Its goal is rehabilitation —enabling an individual to live as useful a life as possible despite some degree of chronic impairment.

PREVENTION OF MENTAL ILLNESS: ADAPTATION OF THE PUBLIC HEALTH MODEL

The public health classification system of primary, secondary, and tertiary prevention was adapted for use by the National Institute of Mental Health (NIMH) for a comprehensive review of mental health programs in 1968 (Sobey, 1970). Treatment for the already seriously disturbed was classified as tertiary prevention. Identifying children and adults who showed beginning signs of disturbance, and for whom prompt diagnosis and treatment might ward off more serious mental illness, was labeled secondary prevention. Providing services for the general public that were calculated to reduce the incidence of mental and social problems was called primary prevention.

These levels have since been defined in various ways by different authorities. There is considerable overlap of prevention levels, and most preventive efforts do not fall clearly into any specific category (Clarizio & McCoy, 1983).

THREE LEVELS OF SUICIDE PREVENTION

In yet another adaptation of the public health model, Shneidman (1969, 1970c) has described the three levels of suicide prevention as prevention, intervention, and postvention—those helpful activities that take place before, during, and after a suicidal event. Prevention (primary prevention) involves the sensitization of both professionals and the general public to the problem of suicide; the early identification of individuals and groups at risk; the availability of services; dissemination of information, particularly about warning signs; and the lowering of cultural taboos so that suicidal individuals would ask for help. Ideally, this level of prevention would also include such major societal changes as freedom from congenital defects, optimal parent-child relations, and a benign social and cultural environment. Intervention (secondary prevention) would include early detection of signs of suicidal intent, referral to agencies and resources within the community, and the provision of both crisis intervention and long-term treatment for the individual in distress. Postvention (tertiary prevention) consists of (a) working with a suicidal individual after an attempt or threat for the purpose of reducing the probability of additional suicidal behavior or (b) working with the survivors of a suicide to help them with their feelings of grief, anger, guilt, and shame (Shneidman, 1969, 1970c).

PRIMARY PREVENTION: A PROACTIVE APPROACH FOR THE SCHOOL

Clarizio and McCoy (1983) have suggested that the school should provide for primary prevention of all types of behavioral disorders by addressing the needs of normal children as well as those with special problems. As reasons for their position, they cite (a) the extensiveness of mental health problems in children and adolescents, (b) the continuing shortage of mental health professionals, and (c) the dubious value of most treatment approaches. Their rationale relates directly to the need for primary prevention of suicidal behavior, which cannot be logically separated from other serious behavior problems, because of the following:

1. Suicidal behavior is prevalent among children with psychiatric disorders, and 12 million children in the United States suffer from mental illness (American Mental Health Fund, 1986).
2. Many depressed or suicidal youngsters, for a variety of reasons, are not brought to the attention of mental health professionals (Kauffman, 1985; Knoblock, 1983).
3. Many children who have committed suicide exhibited no signs of emotional problems beforehand.
4. The number of trained mental health professionals has not kept pace with the increase in need.
5. Treatment approaches are rarely subjected to adequate evaluation, especially regarding their effectiveness with suicidal children and adolescents.

Most of the suicide prevention activity that has taken place in the schools has been secondary or tertiary in nature, consisting of intervention (detection and referral of students who are already exhibiting problems) or tertiary (procedures for dealing with the aftermath of a suicide). An important task now facing the school is to move from the reactive approach of secondary and tertiary prevention of youth suicide to a proactive approach of primary prevention. This is not to suggest that the school should discontinue its efforts to detect the signs of depression and suicidal intent in students and provide assistance for those who are already in distress, but rather that the school should also promote programs of psychological wellness. There is a critical need for interventions that address the problems of children and adolescents before the onset of suicidal behavior. The focus of school programs should be on promoting health as well as on curing disease.

PART II
Suicide Prevention
in the School

13. The School Plan for Suicide Prevention

The first step in establishing an effective school-based program is the development of a comprehensive plan that includes provisions for primary, secondary, and tertiary prevention. Policies and procedures should be established for the school or district that clearly delineate (a) the appropriate steps to follow in the event of a student's suicidal behavior (what should be done and the order in which the steps will be carried out) and (b) the responsibilities of the various school or district personnel in carrying out the plan—the specific person or persons responsible for the actions. A comprehensive school plan will include procedures (a) for the aftermath of a completed suicide (tertiary prevention); (b) for other kinds of suicidal behavior—attempts, threats, and ideation (secondary prevention); and (c) for the enhancement of mental health (primary prevention).

The following procedures or components should be addressed in the plan for secondary and tertiary prevention:

1. Detection of signs of depression or suicidal intent.
2. Assessment of a student's potential for suicide.
3. Crisis intervention, including emergency assistance.
4. Communicating with a student in crisis.
5. Communicating with parents or guardians.
6. Referral to school services or personnel.
7. Assisting parents with referral to community agencies.
8. Making services available in the school or community.
9. Working with community agencies.
10. Working with the media.
11. Liaison with treatment providers.
12. Follow-up activity after a suicide attempt.
13. Procedures to follow in the event of a completed suicide.
14. Training for faculty, staff, parents, and volunteers.
15. Providing information to students.

Members of the planning committee or task force may find other provisions necessary or desirable. No reasonable suggestion should be ignored.

Plans must also be made for the promotion of psychological wellness (primary prevention). The tragedy of youth suicide has focused attention on the serious problems of young people in this generation. Planning for suicide prevention must include measures for meeting the basic needs of children and adolescents—in the home, school, and community.

WHO SHOULD DEVELOP THE PLAN?

The development of the school plan for suicide prevention should be a team effort by all individuals, groups, and agencies that may be affected by its implementation. Because the program must reflect the needs and concerns of students, parents, faculty, staff, and the community, representatives from all of these groups should have a voice in its development. Among school personnel that should be involved are classroom teachers, special educators, psychologists, social workers, school nurses, counselors, administrators (school and district), school board members, cafeteria workers, bus drivers, custodians, and other members of the staff. Anyone who might come in contact with a suicidal child should be invited to participate.

Those responsible for the development of prevention strategies must be knowledgeable about services and agencies that are currently available in the school and community, so that the plan will reflect only strategies that are feasible. For example, it is not only useless but possibly harmful to refer potentially suicidal individuals to private practitioners that they cannot afford or to community agencies that cannot furnish the necessary services. Representatives from the following community services, agencies, and organizations should be invited to be members of the planning committee: mental health associations, health and human services, crisis centers, medical clinics, hospitals, psychiatric facilities, counseling centers, law enforcement, courts, correctional institutions, television stations, newspapers, churches and other religious groups, volunteer organizations, and survivors groups. There may be others that should be included. Depending on the size of the community, there may be more, fewer, or different organizations and agencies with an interest in the welfare of children and youth.

Community leaders should be involved in developing the plan. If the services available in the community are inadequate, the planning group should establish priorities for the addition of agencies or personnel. Influential members of the community can be of great assistance in procuring additional services. Administrators and elected or appointed officials at the community, state, province, or national level should therefore be encouraged to participate in the planning.

GOALS, OBJECTIVES, SERVICES, RESPONSIBILITIES, AND EVALUATION

A special education model can be applied to a comprehensive plan for suicide prevention as well as to the needs of an individual student. Special educators are well versed in the requirements of an Individual Educational Plan (IEP). A plan for suicide prevention should be similar to an IEP. It should include (a) identified needs; (b) long-term and short-term goals; (c) changes that must be made in curriculum, methods, and services; (d) the identification of individuals or agencies who will provide those services; and (e) methods for evaluating the outcomes of those services. The plan must also be subjected to continuous reevaluation and modification when necessary or desirable. As we learn more about youth suicide, we must make changes accordingly in programs aimed at prevention. The planning committee's work may never be finished.

This text focuses primarily on the school's responsibility in preventing youth suicide. The responsibilities of other institutions will therefore be addressed from the standpoint of the school as the pivotal agency. This is not intended in any way to belittle the importance of the family, the community, or society; it is rather an attempt to explain what the educator should know, and what the school can do, in preventing this tragedy.

14. Assessment of Suicide Potential

When a student has exhibited signs of depression or suicidal intent, it is crucial to determine, to the greatest extent possible, whether there is an imminent danger of suicide. This assessment should be made by a team of school personnel (not by a teacher or school counselor alone) and must not be considered as a replacement for evaluation by mental health professionals. School personnel should always recommend that parents refer the student to a mental health professional for further evaluation.

The determination of an individual's potential for suicide is extremely difficult, if not impossible, even for a highly trained clinician. There is simply no definitive way to know whether an individual might kill himself, but certain factors are generally considered to make appropriate decisions regarding immediate intervention. Any error in judgment should be in the direction of doing too much rather than too little when a child's life may be at stake (Guetzloe, 1987; Guetzloe & Johnson, 1985). Within the school, the following factors should be immediately evaluated by a team of school professionals, in discussion with anyone who may be able to furnish information regarding the student's intent—the student himself, teachers, staff, peers, and parents or guardians:

1. Health and physical condition (illness, debilitating injury, failure of medical treatment).

2. Present emotional state (symptoms of depression or other psychiatric disturbance, agitation, irritability, elation, peacefulness).

3. Family or home situation (broken home; family suicidal behavior; family psychiatric disorder; physical, sexual, or psychological abuse; sibling rivalry; recent quarrel).

4. Other interpersonal relationships (loss or disruption of a love relationship, withdrawal from friends).

5. School or work situation (dropping out of school or extra-

curricular activites, quitting a job, decrease in academic performance).

6. Alcohol or drug abuse.
7. Problems in the community (being arrested, unwanted publicity).
8. Prior suicide attempts.
9. Suicidal gestures, threats, statements, or thoughts.
10. Presence of a suicide plan (lethality, availability, specificity).
11. Presence of a situational crisis.
12. Abrupt, extreme, and obvious change in behavior (even in a more elated, cheerful, upbeat, or peaceful direction).
13. Preoccupation with death (in conversation, writing, or artwork).
14. Making final arrangements (writing a will, saying good-bye verbally or in writing, giving away prized possessions).

WARNING SIGNS OF SUICIDE

Authorities generally agree that many suicides are planned, and that suicidal people often give clues to their imminent actions. According to Shneidman and Mandelkorn (1970), recognizing these clues, which may be verbal, behavioral, or situational, is a vital first step in preventing the loss of life.

Sometimes there are broad hints; sometimes only subtle changes in behavior. But the suicide decision is usually not impulsive. Most often, it is premeditated. Although it might be done on impulse, and to others seem capricious, in fact, suicide usually is a decision that is given long consideration. (Shneidman & Mandelkorn, 1970, p. 133)

According to the American Association of Suicidology (1977), of the symptoms previously listed, the following are the signs of most immediate danger:

1. Extreme changes in behavior.
2. Signs of depression.
3. A previous suicide attempt.
4. Suicidal threats or statements.
5. Making final arrangements.

There are other overt actions, such as hoarding of medication or purchasing a weapon, that are indications of potential suicide. Among the most crucial is the presence of a detailed, feasible, and lethal suicide plan.

Presence of a Suicide Plan

Suicide plans may range from thinking about how one might kill oneself to having a loaded gun in hand. School personnel should not be afraid to question a suicidal student directly about his suicide plan. Questioning may serve to postpone or prevent suicide, rather than to precipitate such action. The discussion should focus on the specificity of details, the level of lethality, and whether the means and the opportunity are currently available.

Questioning the Suicidal Student. Questions to be asked include the following:

1. Are you planning to hurt yourself?
2. Are you planning to kill yourself?
3. How do you plan to do this?
4. When are you going to do it?
5. Do you already have a weapon?

If the information must be gathered from a family member, friend, or other informant, the following questions should be considered: Has the youngster verbalized that he intends to shoot himself? Are guns available in the home? Has he made overt gestures, such as purchasing a weapon 'or hoarding medication? Does he have the opportunity? Is he usually alone during nonschool hours?

The general rule is that the more specific the plan, the more imminent the suicidal act. This is, however, not always the case, because many suicides appear to be impulsive, taking place without an apparent plan.

Issue of Lethality. A suicide method is considered to have a high level of lethality if its application is likely to result in instantaneous death or, if a slow-acting method is used, there is evidence that special precautions have been taken to ensure success (Shaffer, 1974; Shaffer & Fisher, 1981). Methods are considered to have a low potential for lethality if the methods are unlikely to result in rapid death or if the children have taken active steps to inform other people of their suicidal behavior so that they can be rescued (Shaffer & Fisher, 1981).

Presence of a Situational Crisis

Many events that have triggered suicidal acts may appear to be trivial to an adult, but to a young person the problems seem insurmountable. Further, while a suicidal act may seem impulsive, the youngster may have been in a state of despair for some time. There is particular danger when several of these stressful events occur at the same time, or when one seems to cause others to happen. The proverbial "straw that breaks the camel's back" may result in the death of a child (Guetzloe, 1987; Guetzloe & Johnson, 1985).

Any situation or event that contributes to feelings of low self-worth, loss, humiliation, helplessness, or hopelessness has the potential for precipitating suicidal behavior. Teachers, family, and classmates may often be aware of stressful events to which the child has been subjected in the home, school, or community. A list and discussion of precipitating events is included in Part I of this text.

Extreme Changes in Behavior

Many clinicians have pointed out the importance of recognizing any abrupt change in mood or behavior. The change can be in the direction of a sudden worsening of depression, including symptoms of hopelessness, or even in increased activity (or euphoria).

When a depressed individual is beginning to show signs of apparent improvement, he may be in even more danger than before (Shneidman, 1970b). Many authorities have noted that most suicides related to depression occur within a period of from a few days to 3 months after the individual has made an apparent turn for the better. Any significant change in behavior, even one that looks like improvement, should be assessed as a possible danger sign.

> A 17-year-old champion golfer hanged himself after school in an empty classroom. He was described by classmates, school officials, and teammates as a talented student who set stringent standards for himself. He was never satisfied with his performance in either academics or athletics. He was also described as a loner, sensitive to other people's needs and willing to help, but never very close to others. He had been diagnosed as clinically depressed and was in treatment. He was reported to be improving.

According to an expert in family therapy, problems in treatment or therapy should also be considered as danger signs of suicidal potential (Richman, 1986). Negative or fearful attitudes about treatment or reaching an impasse in therapy may result in a young person's becoming increasingly suicidal.

Signs of Depression

According to Blumenthal (cited in Tugend, 1984), the early detection and treatment of depression is the single most important preventive strategy for youth suicide. The diagnosis of depression, however, is

(a) extremely difficult, even for highly trained psychiatrists, and (b) still a subject of considerable professional debate. Teachers, counselors, and other school personnel are therefore not expected to diagnose depression in young people, but recognition of the symptoms, especially those that are evident in school, is important. Criteria for the diagnosis of depressive disorders, which are included in the revised third edition of the *Diagnostic and Statistical Manual of Mental Disorders* (third edition, revised), commonly called the *DSM-III-R* (American Psychiatric Association, 1987), are listed in the following discussion.

Major Depressive Disorder. One of the symptoms that must be present for a diagnosis of major depressive episode is the presence of either a depressed mood or the loss of interest or pleasure. At least five of the following nine symptoms must have been evident nearly every day for at least 2 weeks and must represent a change from previous functioning:

1. Depressed or irritable mood.
2. Loss of enjoyment or interest in normally pleasurable activities (apathy, in young children).
3. Change in weight, appetite, or eating habits (or failure to make expected weight gains).
4. Problems with sleeping (insomnia or hypersomnia).
5. Psychomotor agitation or retardation (hyperactivity, in children).
6. Loss of energy or feelings of fatigue.
7. Feelings of worthlessness or excessive or inappropriate guilt.
8. Diminished ability to attend, think, or concentrate (or indecisiveness).
9. Recurrent thoughts of death or suicide.

Dysthymic Disorder. For a diagnosis of dysthymic disorder, symptoms of depression that are not of sufficient severity and duration to meet the criteria for major depressive disorder may have been present for a period of 1 year. There could be occasional periods of normal mood for no more than 2 months at a time (American Psychiatric Association, 1987).

Disruptive Behavior As a Warning Sign. According to the American Academy of Pediatrics (cited in Mason, 1985), most suicidal adolescents show some kind of disruptive behavior before the suicidal act. Provoking fights, playing with fire, driving recklessly, or petty thievery may be indications of self-destructive behavior (Schrut,

1964). They may exhibit boredom, apathy, hyperactivity, or physical complaints; they may be defiant and delinquent; and they may abuse drugs or alcohol. These and other similar symptoms were once referred to as "masked depression" (Cytryn & McKnew, 1972, 1974, 1980). Such symptoms are now recognized as age-specific features of a major depressive episode in adolescents.

> In adolescents, negativistic or frankly antisocial behavior and use of alcohol or illicit drugs may be present . . . . Feelings of wanting to leave home or of not being understood and approved of, restlessness, grouchiness, and aggression are common. Sulkiness, a reluctance to cooperate in family ventures, and withdrawal from social activities, with retreat to one's room, are frequent. School difficulties are likely. There may be inattention to personal appearance and increased emotionality, with particular sensitivity to rejection in love relationships. (American Psychiatric Association, 1987, p. 220)

Signs of Suicide Potential in Depressed Individuals. Litman (1970) has listed four characteristics or situations as "ominous signs of suicide potentiality in depressives" (p. 303): impatience; a detailed, feasible, lethal suicide plan; pride, suspicion, and hyperindependence as character traits; and withdrawal or isolation. Isolation should be considered as a possibile danger sign if the individual is living with someone who is so emotionally removed from him that the arrangement is, in effect, like living alone.

Previous Suicide Attempt

A student who has made a prior suicide attempt is at great risk for further attempts, which may become increasingly lethal. Information about previous attempts is generally not readily available. It is most easily obtained by simply asking the student.

Suicidal Threats or Statements

Suicidal threats or statements (verbal clues) may be direct or indirect. Some are obvious, such as, "I wish I were dead," or "I am tired of living." Others are more subtle, such as "No one cares whether I live or die," or "Things will never get any better." Teachers may hear remarks related to school, such as "Don't bother to grade my final—I won't be here for the report card," or questions such as "How does it feel to die?" or "How do you leave your body to science?"

Making Final Arrangements

A common sign of imminent suicide is the act of settling affairs and "getting the house in order" (Guetzloe & Johnson, 1985). Youngsters may bring prized possessions—record collections, pictures, or clothing—to school and give them to their friends. They may write their wills or letters of farewell. They may apologize to classmates they think they have wronged. In retrospect, people have noted that these arrangements are like those of a person who is going on a long trip. The suicidal student is, in effect, saying good-bye.

Preoccupation with Death

Many normal, nonsuicidal children and adolescents may be preoccupied with death, particularly those that have recently experienced the death of a family member, friend, or pet. This preoccupation may be evidenced in the youngster's artwork, creative writing, or choice of music and reading material. There are gradations, however, in the intensity of children's preoccupations with death; suicidal children are most intensely so preoccupied, often thinking of death as both reversible and pleasant (Pfeffer, 1983, 1986). Pfeffer (1986) has suggested that intense preoccupation with death in any child should be considered a warning sign of possible suicidal tendencies.

NEED FOR FURTHER EVALUATION OF THE SUICIDAL STUDENT

This chapter's discussion is not an exhaustive list of the possible signs of suicidal behavior; neither is the presence of any of these signs necessarily an indication that the student is contemplating suicide. A sudden onset of one or more of these symptoms, however, should be considered serious enough to call for special assistance for the youngster. School intervention should include immediate notification of the parents or guardians (as well as designated school personnel) and referral to appropriate individuals or agencies for further evaluation.

A CAVEAT ABOUT SCREENING

Screening the entire student population for depression or suicidal behavior is ill-advised. The use of general surveys or risk assessment instruments in the school or classroom is not only ineffective but may, in fact, be harmful for the following reasons:

1. Mental health professionals have reported that such screenings result in a large number of "false positives," in that many children may be identified as being suicidal when they are not. Conversely, there is also the possibility of the "false negative," which could result in a suicidal child not being referred for further evaluation. Many suicides, especially among young people, are impulsive acts. Hawton, Cole, O'Grady, and Osborn (1982) found that 50% of a group of adolescent self-poisoners had thought seriously about the act for less than 15 minutes, and another 16% had thought about it for between 15 minutes and one hour. Taylor and Stansfield (1984) found that three-fourths of a group of adolescent self-poisoners contemplated their actions for less than 2 hours. A child could respond that he was not suicidal on one day and commit suicide the next.

2. There is the ever present danger of contagion. No material should ever be presented to students that makes suicidal behavior appear to be acceptable. Particularly objectionable are those questionnaires that ask students to list (or choose) the reasons they might kill themselves or the methods that they would use. Such instruments have no place in the classroom. They are especially dangerous to children who may already have emotional problems, as discussed in Chapter 19.

3. Authorities are in general agreement that the most effective method for assessing suicidal risk within the school setting is a simple questioning procedure conducted by someone who has already established a relationship with the child, as discussed above. The use of a questionnaire during the interview may even give the impression to the child that the adult is more interested in filling in the blanks than in understanding the problem.

4. Such instruments have been criticized as violations of the Protection of Pupil Rights Amendment (Section 439 of the General Education Provisions Act, 20 U.S. Code Section 1232h), also known as the Hatch Amendment (Schlafly, 1985). Parents have complained that questionnaires are not only upsetting to their children, but are also an invasion of privacy.

15. Crisis Intervention in the School

Suicidal behavior ranges on a continuum that includes completed suicides, attempts, threats, gestures, verbalizations, or thoughts. Students may also exhibit signs of depression without apparent suicidal intent. With the exception of the crisis caused by a completed suicide, the procedures for school personnel to follow are somewhat similar for all of these situations, with the major differences related to the amount of time available for determining appropriate actions. In the case of suicidal ideation, there is probably time to ponder; in the case of a serious attempt, emergency procedures must be implemented without delay. Guidelines are discussed here for (a) procuring emergency assistance following a suicide attempt, (b) crisis intervention during a suicide threat, (c) communicating with a suicidal student, (d) intervention with students who verbalize suicidal intent, and (e) steps to follow when students exhibit signs of depression without apparent suicidal intent.

STEPS TO FOLLOW IN CRISIS INTERVENTION

The following order is suggested for the implementation of the school crisis intervention plan:

1. Observation of signs of depression or suicidal behavior in the student.
2. Immediate determination of potential for suicide.
3. Emergency assistance, if an attempt has been made or seems imminent.
4. Evaluation of available support systems.
5. Notification of family, other supportive individuals, and appropriate school or district personnel.
6. Referral to school or community services.
7. Resolution of immediate crisis and planning for follow-up services.

8. Implementation of planned program and provision of school or community services.
9. Establishment of supportive structure.
10. Long-term follow-up in home, school, and community.

These steps are briefly explained in this chapter.

Observation of Signs of Depression or Suicidal Behavior

School personnel who see students on a daily basis may be the first to recognize behaviors that may be indicators of suicidal intent. Behaviors exhibited by a suicidal student may include withdrawal from friends and social groups, quitting a job, dropping out of extracurricular activities, quitting team sports, a decline in class participation, failure to complete assignments, inattentiveness, truancy, or uncharacteristic rule breaking. A very important danger sign is any extreme change in behavior. Symptoms of depression and other warning signs are further discussed in Chapter 14.

Immediate Determination of Potential for Suicide

If a suicide attempt is in progress or the student is threatening suicide, emergency procedures must be implemented without delay. If the student is verbalizing intent or shows signs of depression or severe emotional distress without verbalizing intent, the individual who has witnessed the behavior should report immediately to the school crisis team. The student should be kept under close supervision and should not be allowed to leave the school until the parent or the parent's designated representative has been notified and provisions have been made for an adult to continue supervision. Supervision is a critical provision. The student must not be left alone.

Procuring Emergency Assistance Following Suicide Attempt

If a suicide attempt occurs at school or during a school activity away from the campus, school staff must immediately provide for the physical safety of the student by administering first aid or securing emergency medical or mental health treatment. The names and work stations of school personnel who have been trained in first aid or cardiopulmonary resuscitation should be listed for each member of the faculty and staff.

Emergency Medical Assistance. All school personnel should also be familiar with the emergency services that are available in the community, which generally include the following:

1. Emergency medical services (paramedics).
2. Fire department rescue squad.
3. Ambulance services.
4. Law enforcement agencies.
5. Poison control center.
6. Hospitals.
7. Walk-in clinics.

Telephone numbers and addresses of these and any other emergency services should be readily available at every telephone station on campus, as well as in school vehicles, so that assistance can be summoned immediately. In a life-threatening situation, highly trained paramedics (emergency medical services) would be the preferred choice. These individuals can begin medical treatment on the way to the emergency room, which may often make the difference between life and death for the victim. Fire department rescue squad personnel are trained in lifesaving procedures, as are law enforcement agents. The choices for an individual school may often depend on the proximity of the emergency unit to the school as well as the nature of the emergency. Calling for emergency services must not be delayed while efforts are being made to contact the parents or guardians. Medical treatment for a minor child is generally mandated—not only by common sense but also by law. As soon as emergency assistance has been summoned, the principal or designated representative, the parent or guardian, and other school or district personnel should be informed.

Emergency Assistance for a Suicide Threat. A student may threaten suicide and present a life-threatening situation on the school grounds or during an off-campus school activity. In this instance, law enforcement agents, emergency mental health personnel, and emergency medical services should be contacted immediately. Until they arrive, school personnel should stay with the student, keeping him in sight and within voice contact at all times. The student must not be left alone. If there is a teacher or other member of the staff available with whom the student has already established a positive relationship, that person could be summoned to assist. Again, parents must be notified, as well as the responsible persons within the school or district.

What if no other assistance is available? Although such situations are rare, a teacher or member of the staff may encounter a suicide crisis when there is not enough time to call a professional or when emergency services are not available. Such crises have occurred at school and during school excursions. In this instance, it is crucial to communicate appropriately and buy time until other help is available or the young person makes the decision to live.

Authorities have often suggested that, even when a suicidal person is standing on a high window ledge or pointing a gun at himself, he is still ambivalent regarding the wish to live or die (Shneidman, 1970b). There is still a chance for life if anyone can provide hope. A potential rescuer of a suicidal youngster must remain calm and supportive, and any statements made must be positive in nature. The most important considerations are to rekindle hope and postpone the suicidal act. If another person who is more experienced in crisis intervention should arrive, the one who has been talking with the suicidal student should not leave, but should rather introduce the new person and stay close by to assist. It is important that the student does not feel rejected or deserted by anyone at this critical time.

Communicating with a Student Who Is Threatening Suicide. The manner in which a potential rescuer communicates with a youngster who is threatening suicide is extremely important. Guidelines for communicating with a student during such a situation are as follows:

1. Remain calm. Speak gently, quietly, and carefully.
2. If the student does not know you, introduce yourself and say that you are there to help.
3. Verbalize concern. Tell the youngster, "I care about you."
4. If the student has a lethal weapon or substance, gently ask him to give it up, dispose of it, or put it away. Crisis counselors have suggested such statements as, "Please put down the gun so that we can talk," "Please flush the pills down the toilet so that we can talk," or "I want you to leave the gun here and come into the other room so we can talk."
5. Ask questions such as, "Can we talk about this?" "Can you tell me about this problem?" "Can you think of any other ways to solve this problem?" "Has this ever happened before?" "How did you deal with it then?"
6. Do not be judgmental. This is not the time to deliver a sermon. Do not tell the student that he is being selfish or not thinking of others. A suicidal person does not need more guilt. Further, do not make comments about the terrible effect his suicide would have on family and friends. That may be precisely the motivation for the act.
7. Reinforce any comments that seem positive or hopeful in nature, especially regarding any alternatives to suicide.

8. Do not try to pressure or hurry him to make a decision. Tell him that you want to help, that you want him to live, and that you will not leave him.
9. Do not give up. Keep reminding the youngster that there are many people who care and who are available to help. The longer he stays alive, the greater are the chances that other helpers will become available or that he will make his own decision to live.

As soon as there is another person available to make the call, help should be requested from emergency medical and mental health services. The potential rescuer should not be misled by a young person's promises that the danger is over. A youngster who threatens suicide must not be left alone.

Calling Parents to the Scene. If there are any indications that the student is seeking revenge against the parents, or that the parent/child relationship is the cause of the suicidal threat, the parents should be summoned but kept out of sight of the suicidal student until the emergency workers determine that their presence will be helpful rather than harmful. The arrival of parents on the scene might precipitate a suicide completion.

Intervention with Students Who Verbalize Suicidal Intent. If the crisis does not constitute an actual attempt, but there are verbalizations or other indications of suicidal intent by the student, parents or guardians must be notified and the student should be closely supervised until the parent or the parent's designated representative can assume responsibility. Students who verbalize suicidal intent must not be left alone, even for a brief period. The seriousness of the situation and the necessity for obtaining professional help for the student should be conveyed to the parent or other adult in charge. School personnel should offer assistance in contacting appropriate resources and maintain contact with the parents to be sure that assistance has been obtained as well as sought.

Intervention with Students Who Exhibit Signs of Depression. A student may be exhibiting signs of depression without actually verbalizing intent to commit suicide. In this case, parents should be informed; and school personnel may meet to discuss appropriate interventions. If it is determined that school problems are contributing to the student's feelings of depression, some change in the student's school program would be in order. The school should also accept the responsibility for maintaining contact with the parents or guardians to monitor improvement or deterioration in the student's behavior.

Parents must always be informed immediately unless it is evident that abuse is a factor in the student's suicidal behavior, as discussed previously. In the case of abuse or neglect, the law generally provides for reporting to protective services.

The symptoms of depression are listed in Chapter 14. According to the American Psychiatric Association (1987), if these symptoms are evident for a period of more than 2 weeks, the parent should seek psychiatric evaluation for the student. Again, school personnel should offer assistance in contacting community resources and should make sure that the contact has been made and that services for the child have been procured.

Notifying Parents, Other Agencies, and School Personnel

In the case of a suicide attempt, parents or guardians must be notified immediately, unless there are indications that the student has been abused by the parents. In that case, provisions should be made for the child's protection, as further discussed in the following sections.

A current listing of telephone numbers and work addresses at which parents or guardians may be located should already be available within the school. The necessity for a system for communicating with parents or guardians is further discussed in the sections of this text on intervention in the aftermath of a suicide.

Providing a School Contact Person. The principal may designate a counselor, school psychologist, or school nurse to be the person who contacts parents in case of an emergency. It is extremely important that the person who makes an emergency call to a parent or guardian is able to deal with this kind of situation in a calm, helpful, and professional manner. The school contact person should be (a) knowledgeable about school and community resources and (b) immediately available (by telephone) during the day to discuss concerns regarding the student's progress or the provision of treatment and services.

Notifying Other Supportive Individuals. Notification of supportive individuals outside of the family may be indicated, especially if there are problems within the family unit. If the student is not living with the family, it may be necessary or desirable to notify other agencies or individuals. Further, there may be other people that would be helpful to the student in crisis—a minister, girlfriend or boyfriend, employer, neighbor, or close friend. The evaluation of the student's available support system and the decision to notify other individuals should be made by the school crisis team, in discussion with those persons who have been in close contact with the student.

Reporting Abuse. There is only one situation in which the parents or guardians are not notified immediately. If there are indications that the student has been abused, the law provides for reporting to protective services or law enforcement agencies. This report should be made before there is a possibility that the hospital or emergency services would release the child to the parents. Reports of additional abuse after a suicide attempt has brought the family to the attention of the school or community agencies are not uncommon.

Notifying School or District Personnel. As soon as possible, established district procedures should be followed for informing the appropriate persons among the school or district staff and faculty. Teachers and other school personnel should be informed of the facts so that they can be of assistance in avoiding panic or contagion.

Referral to School or Community Services

During a workshop for educational personnel on the topic of suicide prevention, the following note was passed to the podium by the supervisor of guidance and counseling services:

> We received a written referral by courier at 4:00 p.m. on Friday. The teacher stated that he was concerned about a certain student [whose name was included] who might be suicidal. The referral was dated 3 days before. Both teacher and student had left town for the weekend. Please tell these people to use the telephone and not the courier.

The point is obvious. Children who might be suicidal should be referred immediately by telephone and not through the usual procedures for requesting student services. Time is of the essence. The child in the situation described above is still alive, having lived through the weekend. The outcome of another case, widely circulated in newspapers across the country, was devastating.

> The 11-year-old was a very intelligent child; and he had worked hard on his essay, writing and rewriting until he had it just the way he wanted it. He called it "Suicide Mistake." It described how an 11-year-old boy suffocated himself by putting a plastic bag over his head.
>
> He turned the essay in on Monday, but his teacher didn't read it until Monday night. Disturbed by what she read, the teacher

immediately called the school principal, and they agreed to seek counseling for the child the following morning.

Even as the teacher and principal talked, paramedics were vainly trying to revive the child. His mother had found him in his room with a plastic bag over his head.

Investigators found that the boy had been seeing a counselor at the local mental health center because he was having difficulties in adjusting to his new school. Teachers had recently reported improvement in his attitude. Investigators found several drafts of the essay in his room.

Referral for Special Education Assessment. If the symptoms of depression appear to be pervasive, exist to a marked degree, and are evident over a period of time, the student may qualify for special education services as provided by law. Parent permission must be obtained for assessment, and the district procedures for such evaluation may be implemented. Additional information regarding special education's role and responsibility may be found in Chapter 19.

Referral to Community Agencies. A number of options may be considered for the provision of treatment or services for a depressed or suicidal student. Referrals to treatment agencies, public or private, are normally the responsibility of the parents. Because most community mental health agencies are not able to accept a child as a client without parent permission, it is highly desirable that the parents make the initial contact with the agency. For a variety of reasons, however—including denial, fear of social stigma, or feelings of guilt—parents may fail to seek professional help, even after being informed by school personnel that the child may be at risk for suicide.

Referral Without Parent Permission. In some districts, health and welfare guidelines may dictate that a minor child will receive treatment for a life-threatening physical or mental illness, with or without parent permission. In those communities, school personnel may notify the proper authorities if the parents refuse to seek assistance for a suicidal child. Before referrals to other agencies are made by school personnel, the parents or guardians must be informed of this decision; and previous attempts to secure their cooperation must be documented.

Procuring Emergency Mental Health Services. A number of options for the provision of emergency mental health services may already be in place in the community. Crisis intervention centers, suicide prevention hotlines, and law enforcement agencies in any geographical area will be able to provide current information on local services.

A recent addition to emergency mental health services in many communities is the crisis stabilization unit, which provides a brief and intensive intervention for both adults and children. Its purpose is either to return the individual to the community (with appropriate counseling or psychiatric care) or to secure placement in a hospital or other mental health facility. The crisis stabilization unit usually works in close cooperation with law enforcement agencies to provide immediate and effective services. Services provided include a suicide prevention hotline, mental health assessment, crisis counseling, referral for immediate placement, admission to a mental health facility, and initiation of treatment planning. Trained personnel provide access or referral to other community health services, alcohol and drug abuse programs, inpatient hospitalization, and social services.

Provisions for Involuntary Examination. In some states (e.g., Florida), the law provides for involuntary examination and subsequent hospitalization of individuals who are in danger of harming themselves or others. This examination may be initiated, under certain conditions, by a law enforcement officer, by a licensed mental health professional (such as a psychiatrist, clinical psychologist, or psychiatric social worker), or by family members (or other concerned individuals) through court action. If a licensed professional witnesses a suicide attempt or is present during a suicide threat, involuntary examination procedures may be initiated.

Certain criteria must be met before involuntary examination may be initiated, such as the following:

1. There is reason to believe that the person is mentally ill.

2. The individual has refused voluntary examination after an explanation of the purpose of the examination.

3. The individual is unable to make the determination that examination is necessary.

4. The lack of care or treatment poses a real threat of substantial harm to the individual's well-being.

5. There is substantial likelihood that, without care or treatment, the individual will cause serious bodily harm to either himself or others, as evidenced by recent behavior.

Provision of Counseling, Therapy, or Treatment

Among community resources that are generally available for treating or counseling a suicidal individual are psychiatric hospitals; community mental health centers; private psychiatrists, psychologists, and counselors; youth services; child protection teams; and other health and human service agencies. Although some of these options are costly, there are often services available that charge according to the family's ability to pay. It is crucial that school personnel be willing to work with parents in seeking assistance that they can afford for the suicidal child. Treatment options are further discussed in Part I of this text.

Follow-up with a Suicidal Student

After the immediate crisis has been resolved, a suicidal youngster will still require supervision and services for an extended period of time. Provisions for follow-up services are extremely important, because suicidal youth may be at risk for several years following an attempt or threat. Many suicides occur on the anniversary of a previous attempt. Further attempts may also occur when there is a lessening of attention because parents, teachers, counselors, and friends believe that the student is no longer in danger. An individualized intervention plan should be developed for a depressed or suicidal student that includes the following provisions (Guetzloe, 1987):

1. Some immediate and positive change in the student's life—at home, at school, or in the community.
2. Provision of therapy, counseling, and/or contact with supportive individuals in the family, school, or community.
3. Continuing supervision and support in the home and school until (as determined by the treatment provider) there is no longer any danger of suicide.
4. Delivery of whatever has been promised.

The preceding discussion has focused on the steps for school personnel to follow in the event of (a) a suicide attempt; (b) a suicidal threat, gesture, or verbalization of intent; or (c) the detection of signs of depression in a student. Additional information regarding the essential components of a school suicide prevention plan will be found in the following chapters.

16. Working with Parents in Preventing Youth Suicide

Many of the risk factors and precipitating events associated with youth suicide have been related to family history or family interactions. The importance of the family in this regard must not be underestimated. It is extremely important, however, that school personnel do not imply in any way that the parents are to blame for the problems of a depressed or suicidal child. Parents must be encouraged to use the school as a resource, and they must be treated with courtesy and respect. This section provides information that school personnel can share with parents specifically regarding the problem of youth suicide and the development and implementation of a school-based suicide prevention program.

COMMUNICATING WITH PARENTS OR GUARDIANS

One of the primary responsibilities of the school is to establish communication links with parents or guardians. As previously mentioned, a system for communicating quickly with parents or guardians is essential to the effectiveness of a school crisis plan. The telephone numbers of the parents (or another adult who could assume responsibility for a student) should be readily available. The school parent organization or a cadre of volunteers could be helpful in developing the system and keeping the listings current. Educators are well aware that the school cannot always depend on the students to furnish this information; some students would prefer that school personnel do not have immediate access to their parents.

Children may not exhibit the same behaviors at home that have been noticed at school. Parents may not be aware of a student's problems with school, teachers, or peers. Parents must be notified immediately of changes in behavior or signs of emotional problems so that they may provide (or seek) assistance.

On the other hand, problems may be evident at home that have not been noticed at school. Parents should also be encouraged to use the school as a resource and to notify teachers, counselors, or other school personnel when a child shows signs of emotional distress.

PARENT INVOLVEMENT IN PLANNING AND TRAINING FOR SUICIDE PREVENTION

Parents should be invited to participate in both the development of the school suicide prevention plan and the training that is made available to the faculty, staff, and volunteers. They should also be invited to review instructional materials on the topic of suicide that will be used in the classroom. Parents have often expressed concern regarding the content of course material used in suicide prevention programs. Their approval and support is extremely important; they must be kept informed.

WHAT PARENTS OF A DEPRESSED OR SUICIDAL CHILD NEED TO KNOW

Suicidal young people need a great deal of support from the family, and families must be given assistance in understanding the needs of a suicidal child. They need correct information as well as therapy.

One of the most important things for parents to know is that depressed and suicidal young people respond favorably to evidence of caring, concern, and efforts toward understanding their problems. It is extremely important that parents listen to their children. If listening, understanding, and expressions of concern do not seem to improve the situation, then parents should quickly seek professional help.

If the child's problem seems to be related to school, the school counselor would be a good resource for parents. In a crisis situation, an immediate referral should also be made to a mental health professional, and the school contact person or crisis team can assist with this process. The student's teachers and other school personnel should also be informed so that they can provide support and supervision for a student in distress.

Asking for Help

Parents should be advised of their responsibility to secure intervention or treatment for a depressed or suicidal child. They should provide appropriate models for their child by seeking professional assistance when it is needed. The importance of this cannot be overemphasized. Many young people think that asking for help is a sign of weakness.

Responding to Suicidal Behavior

A 15-year-old girl shot herself in the abdomen during an agriculture class at a junior high school. Police said that she had brought the 22-caliber handgun to school from her home. The girl was listed in stable condition at the local hospital.

The girl's stepfather said that she was upset about problems with her boyfriend. Her mother said that the shooting "wasn't really a suicide attempt . . . she just wanted attention."

It is crucial that parents understand that all suicidal behavior must be taken seriously. Ignoring or belittling suicidal verbalizations or actions may be interpreted by the young person as an "invitation to die" (Jourard, 1969, p. 136). Further, subsequent attempts are likely to occur. A gun is an extremely lethal weapon. Without the desired "attention," a child might choose a gun again—and succeed.

The Right to Question

Parents must also be made aware that they have a right to question the treatment program and to make changes when the child is not showing any signs of progress (or when the child's condition appears to worsen). The following are a father's comments:

If I could live this last week over, I would tell my son to come back home to live. I would tell him not to look for a job until he was ready. Depressed children need time to heal, time to forget the pressures that made them depressed.

He suffered depression for 2 years. He was hospitalized for 6 months. Under medical supervision, antidepressant drugs were tried, one at a time. Every other medical treatment, including electric shock, was tried. He seemed to be getting better.

He went to a halfway house for the next year. He was told to look for work and that, when he got a job, he might be able to move into an apartment with other young men.

He asked to move back home. We thought he was getting better care at the halfway house, so we refused. I asked that he be put back into the hospital, but they said he didn't need a hospital. He was crying out for help, but we didn't understand.

He killed himself a few days ago. I failed my son. I want to keep other parents from making the same mistake. Don't tell your depressed children what you think is best for them. Ask them—and listen.

SUGGESTIONS FOR PARENTS

The following are suggestions for communication and intervention that school personnel can share with parents (Guetzloe, 1987):

1. Listen carefully and encourage your child to communicate. Do not belittle his problems, no matter how trivial they may seem.

2. Verbalize unconditional love, caring, concern, and respect. Don't let your child turn you off. Keep trying and keep listening.

3. Encourage discussion of thoughts and feelings as well as events and people.

4. Practice self-disclosure. Share some of the mistakes you've made and how you coped with the problems. Help your child understand that no one is perfect, and no one is expected to be.

5. Stay in touch with your child. Know who your child's friends are, where he is, and with whom. Show interest in your child's interests.

6. Help your child establish reasonable and attainable goals and expectations—in and out of school.

7. Encourage socialization. In times of crisis, having a friend who may not be the parents' choice is preferable to social isolation.

8. Assist with peer conformity. Help to correct typical problems—obesity, acne, vision problems, or crooked teeth—that might set the child apart. Adolescents, in particular, need to conform (within reason and the law) to their peers' dress and hair styles.

9. Let the child choose outside activities. Don't "overprogram" with music lessons, martial arts, and a job.

10. Encourage problem-solving, decision-making, and independence.

11. Help the child learn tolerance for failure, difficulty, and frustration. A child should not be punished for making a mess, but rather taught how to clean it up.

12. Praise the child and show appreciation for his areas of strength. These may be in art, music, mechanics, or lawn care—and not in academics.

13. Don't be afraid to ask for help. There are many individuals and agencies that are available to assist parents when a child is in crisis. Notify the school first; counselors and teachers will help with the rest.

14. If there is any reason to suspect that your child is considering suicide, take charge and mobilize! Dispose of pills, guns, and other weapons; provide close supervision; and get professional help.

17. Guidelines for Counseling a Suicidal Student

The following guidelines (Guetzloe, 1985a, 1985b), are intended for use by teachers, counselors, or other educational personnel who will be communicating directly with a depressed or suicidal student. They are suitable for use in the counselor's or administrator's office or any other private place (not in front of the class). They are not to be used in lieu of notifying parents or guardians or getting other professional help.

1. Never take suicide threats or gestures casually. Don't assume that a student "isn't the type." Do something! Take charge. Mobilize the available resources. According to Weissberg (1983), disregard of suicidal signals may be misinterpreted by suicidal persons as a covert wish that they should carry out their actions.

2. Don't be afraid to bring up the subject. Your discussion will not encourage the student to go through with his plans. On the contrary, it will help him to know that someone cares and is willing to become involved. It may save a life.

3. Question closely and carefully about a possible suicide plan. Ask, "Are you planning to hurt yourself? Have you thought of suicide? How do you plan to kill yourself? Do you have a gun (or pills)? When do you plan to do this?"

4. This is not the time to debate the morality of suicide. Don't preach. As stated by Grollman (1971), "for the suicidal person, self-destruction is not a theological issue; it is the result of unbearable emotional stress" (p. 88).

5. Identify the major stresses or events that have precipitated the suicidal behavior. If you cannot understand what the student is feeling, do not pretend that you do. Say instead, "You seem so troubled. If you tell me how you feel, I might understand."

6. Do not respond with any statements such as," But you have everything to live for," "Think of the things you have that most people don't," or "I can't believe you would think of ending your life." A suicidal youngster is already suffering from tremendous guilt; he does not need to hear that his thoughts are ridiculous.

7. Encourage the student to use other situational supports: parents, friends, ministers, school personnel, neighbors, or a mental health clinic. Let him know that you or another staff person will help to make the necessary contacts.

8. If the suicidal behavior has been precipitated by the loss of a romantic relationship, this is not the time for comments such as, "There are plenty of fish in the sea," "There's another train leaving the station every minute," or any other comment that belittles the importance of the relationship. For the suicidal youngster, the loss of a girlfriend or boyfriend seems to be the end of any hope for a loving relationship. Sharing the terrible pain you felt at the time of a similar loss might be helpful. Some students may have suffered disruptions of homosexual relationships. In such a case, it is extremely important that a potential rescuer does not pass judgment on the appropriateness or the morality of the relationship.

9. Don't leave a suicidal student alone. Stay with him until another adult can assume responsibility. Suicidal youth should be kept under close supervision. They should also be kept out of harm's way to whatever extent possible. A suicidal youngster should not be allowed to participate in potentially lethal activities, such as motorcycling, hang gliding, scuba diving, or mountain climbing. Means of self-destruction are too readily available.

10. Dispose of anything in the immediate environment that could be used as a weapon and remind parents or any other person who is supervising the child to do the same. Such items as guns, drugs, ropes, razors, knives, or toxic chemicals should be placed in locked storage. Leaving weapons in accessible places may be misconstrued by the youngster as an invitation to kill himself.

11. Mention school or community events that will be occurring later in the day, the next day, or next week. Try to get a commitment from the student to attend and participate in these events.

12. Be aware of the student's response to you. If he seems accepting and there has been an improvement in mood, or a commitment to live, continue the present tactics. A suicidal student may often verbalize, "Leave me alone—I don't need your assistance," but the cry for help is still obvious. At such times, the teacher or

counselor simply reaffirms, "I care about you. I want to help. I'll be here for you."

13. Be sure that the student has the telephone number of the crisis center, the suicide hotline, or a member of the school staff. A card is better than a piece of paper. Do not put it in a school book or notebook, as he may not find it there. Stuff it in his pocket.

14. Do not promise to keep a student's suicidal behavior secret. As discussed earlier, a student's suicidal behavior must be reported to either the parents or a community agency, depending on the circumstances or precipitating events. Decisions to notify agencies, rather than the parents, should be made by a building or districtwide committee, not by a teacher or counselor alone.

15. Try to get a commitment from the student that he will not hurt himself, and that, if he feels any kind of suicidal impulse, he will call a teacher, counselor, or hotline worker. Suicide prevention workers working with young people have used such statements as, "Promise me that you won't do anything to hurt yourself unless you call the suicide prevention center first," "Promise me that you will be very careful not to harm yourself in any way," or "Promise me that you will call me if you have any thoughts or feelings that you want to hurt yourself."

16. Write a contract. Some crisis intervention workers have used written contracts to get a commitment from a youngster that he will not commit suicide (Drye, Goulding, & Goulding, 1973). The following is a modification of a contract suggested by Getz, Allen, Myers, and Lindner (1983):

I, _____, agree not to kill myself, attempt to kill myself, or bring any harm to myself during the period from _____ to _____ (dates).

I agree to get enough sleep and to eat regularly and well.

I agree to get rid of things I could use to kill myself.

I agree that if I have a bad time and feel that I might hurt myself, I will call _____ at _____(telephone number) or the Suicide and Crisis Center at _____ (telephone number).

Signed _____

Witness _____

Date _____

FIRST AID FOR THE SUICIDAL STUDENT: A POSITIVE CHANGE

Frederick (1985) has observed that suicidal youngsters suffer from the "Three H's"—haplessness, helplessness, and hopelessness (p. 15). First, they may have suffered a series of misfortunes over which they had little or no control. Following these events, they do not have the internal or external resources to deal with the problems, and finally, feelings of hopelessness ensue and suicide appears to be the only alternative. The immediate tasks of a potential rescuer—teacher, counselor, or therapist—are to provide relief from the feelings of hopelessness, to help the youngster explore alternatives to suicidal behavior, and to instill (in the student) some feeling of being in control.

Just Noticeable Difference

Some positive change in the student's life must be effected immediately, to prove that the situation is not hopeless. Shneidman (1985), who recommended such action for therapists, has called this a "J.N.D."—a "Just Noticeable Difference" (p. 228). According to Shneidman, the focus of intervention should not be on "why" suicide is the individual's choice, but rather on solving problems so that suicide is no longer necessary. Shneidman further suggested catering to both "infantile and realistic idiosyncratic needs" to keep the individual alive.

A student's seemingly insurmountable problems may lie in one or more of his several worlds—in the school, home, peer group, or community. The major stresses that led to the suicidal behavior must be identified, and steps must be taken to reduce pressure from those problems. This may require intervention from other agencies and individuals as well as from school services.

Combatting Hopelessness

Dropping a class, changing a schedule, providing a tutor, or removing a threat of punishment may provide hope for a student who is encountering problems at school. For an exceptional student, a change could be made in his Individual Educational Plan (IEP), so that specific risk factors are addressed or so that he can achieve greater success in his academic program.

A sense of hopelessness, as discussed in the section on risk factors, has been found to be a stronger predictor of suicide than the degree of clinical depression (Beck, et al., 1985). According to many clinicians, dealing with suicidal hopelessness should be the central focus of intervention.

Combatting hopelessness should therefore also be a major consideration in modifying school programs for purposes of suicide prevention. School policies and procedures should be examined with reference to whether they might contribute to a sense of hopelessness. Those that do should be changed.

> The boy was a good student, who had been placed in a class in which he was failing. His grade point average would be ruined, and his choices for college would be limited. He was exhibiting signs of suicidal behavior. When his counselor requested a schedule change for him, the principal's response was "If we changed one student's schedule, we'd have a hundred other requests. One failing grade won't hurt him."

This story had a happy ending. Upon receipt of a written memorandum from the counselor outlining the student's symptoms, the risk of possible suicide, and the principal's responsibility in this regard, the principal reversed her position. The point is that it was possible to make the change. There should not be arbitrary rules against schedule changes, but rather guidelines for conditions under which schedule changes should be made. There are obvious implications for other school procedures as well.

SPECIAL ROLE OF THE SCHOOL COUNSELOR

The school counselor, as discussed previously, can help to save lives by being an advocate for a depressed or suicidal child. The school counselor can also play a very important role by maintaining communication between and among the parents or guardians, peers, treatment providers, teachers and other school personnel, and the suicidal student. If there is no counselor assigned to the school, the principal may designate another member of the faculty or staff to be the contact person. The contact person, as discussed earlier, should be someone who is readily accessible by telephone, who has skills in communicating with adults as well as children, and who is familiar with individuals and agencies that can provide assistance to the suicidal child, his family, and the school.

Documentation of Communication

It is important to ask the parent or guardian of a suicidal child to sign a release of information form that gives permission for school personnel to contact and maintain liaison with the treatment provider and other agencies with which the suicidal student may come in contact. School personnel should document (in writing) every contact—verbal or written—with the parents or guardians, other supportive individuals, and community agencies. If the parents refuse to sign the release form, that decision should also be documented.

School Counselor and Follow-Up

There is a crucial need for continued follow-up after a suicide crisis. A student who has threatened or attempted suicide should be considered at risk, even in the absence of overt suicidal behavior, for a period of up to 2 years (or even longer) after the initial suicidal act. A school counselor can provide valuable continuity in follow-up by planning ahead for appointments with the student at intervals throughout the year. Immediately after the suicidal event, and for several weeks thereafter, the appointments should be scheduled several times a week. The time between appointments can be gradually lengthened to twice a week, once every 4 days, once a week, once every 2 weeks, and so forth. The counselor can also simply stop in the youngster's classroom from time to time, so that it is evident that someone is still concerned. If during that period of time the student moves to another school, the counselor should report the student's suicidal behavior to the counselor or principal of the receiving school. Guidelines for such reporting should be included in the school or district procedures for providing psychological services.

Need for 24-Hour-a-Day Assistance

It is important that a suicidal youngster has the telephone number of a crisis hotline or suicide prevention center. He should be able to contact someone at any time if a suicidal impulse should strike. In the absence of such agencies within the community, the school should consider the establishment of its own hotline or simply provide the telephone numbers of counselors or other adults who would be able to respond in a time of crisis.

Many counselors have commented that students will not seek assistance from school counselors, even when they are in desperate need. Students should be reminded by teachers, administrators, and the counselors themselves that help is available and that discussing problems is not inappropriate. Students, especially boys, must believe that one can still be "macho" and ask for help. Early contact with school counselors when students do not have problems is good practice for later help-seeking when the need may be crucial.

Supervision of In-School Counseling Programs

The counselor may also serve as the contact person and in-school supervisor for suicide prevention programs offered in the school by community agencies. A number of such programs are now in operation. In Ithaca, New York, the local Suicide Prevention and Crisis Service provides a program called "Drop-in Counseling" at four high schools ("Suicide Prevention," 1984). The Wheeler Clinic in Plainville, Connecticut, trains high school students to teach and counsel other students about suicide prevention. After their training, the students make this information available to school children in grades 5 through 8 ("Suicide Prevention," 1984). It should be noted that the outcomes of these programs may not have been carefully evaluated. Counselors can provide valuable assistance by carefully observing the responses of the children involved and by making suggestions for change in the programs if such measures seem to be indicated.

Supervision of Peer Counseling Programs

Peer counselors must also be carefully supervised. If there is a peer counseling program in the school, the young counselors should clearly understand their responsibilities for reporting suicide plans or other kinds of suicidal behavior to adults within the school setting. They should not be expected to carry the burden alone or to communicate directly with the parents of suicidal students.

Advantages and Disadvantages of Peer Counseling Programs

Although authorities agree that adolescents are more likely to turn to a peer than to an adult in a time of crisis, there is a danger in having a fellow student assume the task of being a counselor for a suicidal youngster. Ross (1985) has noted that some of the qualities that make peers the confidants of choice also make them dangerously inadequate as counselors and rescuers for the suicidal adolescent. Their "sacred commitment to keep a confidence, their disinclination—or inability—to actively intervene, and their lack of knowledge regarding what could or should be done makes the awesome responsibility that may be imposed upon them an uncertain responsibility at best" (p. 150).

Keeping a Deadly Secret. In a review of psychological autopsies conducted at a suicide prevention center, Robinson (cited in Ross, 1985) found that, in many cases, a friend had known of the adolescent victim's intent, but would not betray the confidence. In another study,

Robinson (cited in Ross, 1985) found that contacts by teenagers on behalf of friends were often dangerously delayed because of their ambivalence about revealing confidential information or their lack of understanding about the actual risk.

Students need to know what they should say when a suicidal friend asks them to keep such information confidential. Students can simply answer, "I care too much about you to keep this secret," or "I would rather have you alive and angry with me."

Legacy of Responsibility. The person in whom a suicide victim confided will often carry a heavy burden of responsibility and guilt. It is therefore extremely important that school personnel involved in teaching suicide prevention information do not imply in any way that young people are responsible for keeping their friends alive. Their responsibilities are rather to immediately report suicidal threats or actions to a responsibile adult—their parents, the friend's parents, or a member of the school faculty or staff.

Therapists have often commented on the tremendous difficulties encountered in working with suicidal clients. Many therapists, including psychiatrists and clinical psychologists, refuse to work with suicidal individuals. A situation that is too difficult for a highly trained mental health professional should not become a student's responsibility.

Educational, Career, and Vocational Counseling

According to Maris (1981), mental health professionals should come to realize the importance of work and play in preventing suicide. It is also extremely important to recognize the influence of the family, the social environment, and the workplace, as previously discussed, in providing the necessary support for a suicidal student.

The school counselor can be of assistance in helping students (and their parents) to define or redefine goals for school or employment. It may be appropriate for a student, particularly one who is depressed or suicidal, to make the decision against going to college immediately after high school.

Graduation from high school is a trying time for students, and college does not provide relief (Hendin, 1985). There have been many reports of suicide among first-year college students.

Paradoxically, the most suicidal students waited for college to escape from what they regarded as an unbearable home situation, only to discover that they became severely depressed and suicidal when they did get to college. Graduating from college, which symbolized a further break from the past, often exacerbated the situation (Hendin, 1985, p. 32).

SIGNS OF PROGRESS

Follow-up activity should be continued for a considerable period of time after a suicide threat or attempt, and some positive change must be made in the student's life, so that he understands that the situation is not hopeless. It is also important that signs of progress are noted, discussed with treatment providers, and reinforced by individuals who are close to the student. Among the signs of improvement after a suicide threat or attempt are the following (Guetzloe, 1987):

1. Improvement in personal appearance.
2. Increase in alertness, motor activity, and quickness of response.
3. Increase in interest in sports, television, and other current events.
4. Increase or improvement in relationships with peers, family, or other adults.
5. Increase in interest in work or recreational activities.
6. Improvement in academic functioning.
7. Exhibition of humor and the ability to laugh.
8. Fewer symptoms of suicidal behavior.

It should be noted that the appearance of one or more of these signs does not mean that the danger is over. As mentioned above, suicidal behavior may recur. Parents, treatment providers, and educational personnel must continue to work together to provide adequate supervision and intervention long after the immediate crisis has been resolved.

As suggested earlier, the school plan for suicide prevention must be developed through the cooperative efforts of all who would be affected by its implementation. Suggestions in this text can be modified to fit the needs and requirements of the specific school or district. The plan should be promulgated, discussed, modified, and put into place in case of need. It should be planned in a "matter-of-fact" manner, as would be the plans for a fire drill. Within the school setting, more students die of suicide than die by fire (Guetzloe, 1987).

18. Procedures to Follow in the Aftermath of a Suicide

The suicide of a student or faculty member has a profound effect on the students, the faculty and staff, and others in the community. Recent reports on cluster suicides seem to suggest that adolescents are deeply affected by the suicide of a peer or other significant person and that they are at risk of emulating such behavior, particularly if they were close friends of the victim or depressed at the time of the death.

AVOIDING CONTAGION

Carefully planned postvention procedures should be put into place immediately following the suicide of a student or member of the faculty or staff. Although many of the procedures are very similar to those that would be followed in the event of a death caused by an accident or illness, there are certain critical differences related to the possibility of contagion, as follows:

1. Great care must be taken to avoid romanticizing or glorifying a suicide. If possible, suggestions should be made to the media that the news reports should not be on the front page of the newspaper or included in the evening telecast. Every effort should be made to avoid contagion.

2. The act should not be described as courageous or rational. Students' remarks about the victim's courage should be countered with such comments as, "Suicide is not a courageous act. It takes much more courage to live and work through a problem than it does to die. There are many people who would help if they were asked; it takes real courage to ask for assistance." It is crucial to

emphasize that suicide is an error in judgment; there are alternatives to suicidal behavior.

3. The victim should not be eulogized; there should be no in-school memorial services for a suicide victim. The victim's family should be encouraged to hold funeral services after school or during the weekend, so that students would not have a holiday by attending the services.

4. Administrators and faculty should express sorrow that the school has suffered a loss and acknowledge that a normal routine is impossible at such a time, but the school schedule should be disrupted as little as possible. The students should be kept informed, however, of the school's plan for dealing with this crisis. Students realize security from knowing that these procedures are in place. It is also extremely important to put the crisis procedures in effect immediately. Students become extremely upset if the death is apparently being ignored by school personnel.

5. If a suicide occurs in the school building, law enforcement agents must be notified immediately; they, in turn, will notify the coroner or medical examiner and carry out other legally required procedures. Students who may have witnessed the suicide should be sent to the school crisis center (with a counselor or other designated faculty member), and the school plan should be implemented immediately to the greatest extent possible. Faculty and staff must be notified, so that they can assist in allaying fears and keeping students away from that area of the building. As soon as is humanly possible, the area should be put back in order so that no gruesome reminders of the event are evident. If an intercom announcement is deemed necessary, it should be reassuring in nature. Accurate information should then be sent by messenger to all of the faculty and staff as soon as possible. Every effort should be made to avoid panic among the students.

COMPONENTS OF THE SCHOOL PLAN FOR POSTVENTION

Postvention procedures, such as those explained here, should be shared (and reviewed on a regular basis) with the school faculty and staff, district administrators, community agency personnel, volunteers, and parent groups. They include the following procedures (Guetzloe, 1987):

Notifying Faculty

Because suicides of young people most often occur at home or after school hours, the school faculty and staff should be notified as soon as possible. All members of the faculty and staff must be informed so that they will be prepared to deal with the situation.

The "telephone tree" is a useful procedure for disseminating information quickly to a large number of people. Each member of the faculty and staff will have a list of several previously designated persons to notify in the event of an emergency. Every member of the faculty and staff is included on the lists.

Anyone who is notified of the suicide of a student (or faculty member) should immediately notify the principal or other previously designated contact person. The principal (or contact person) will call his assigned contacts, who will in turn call others. This procedure continues until all of the faculty and staff have been informed, which is usually accomplished in a short time. All available facts should be given, which will help to prevent the spreading of incorrect information. The faculty are also notified in this way that there will be a meeting before school begins on the next school day.

The principal should also notify appropriate school district personnel. If there is a district crisis team in place, these individuals can be of valuable assistance to the school during this period.

Notifying School Parent Organization

It is essential that a system for communicating with parents in an emergency is already in place, with persons designated to contact parents who may not be available by telephone.

The principal or contact person can notify certain previously designated parents, who will implement a communication network, such as a telephone tree. Parents should be informed of the possibility of contagion, the need for close supervision of any students who may be seriously affected, and the availability of school and community services if they are needed. An evening meeting may be scheduled for parents and other members of the community, and details of this meeting can be given during the call.

Contacting the Victim's Family

The principal or a member of the faculty who was close to the student should contact the victim's family immediately. It is highly desirable that the family work closely with the school in the aftermath of a suicide. The family may have information regarding the victim's siblings, other young relatives, or close friends that would be extremely important in helping these young people through this crisis. The family should also be encouraged to use the school as a resource for themselves.

The family and the school can work together to make decisions regarding information that will be given to the media. The family should be reassured that confidential information will be protected by the school.

Informing the Media

It is essential that one person—a district administrator, the principal, or a previously designated member of the faculty or staff—will be the contact person for the media. In the event of a suicide, faculty and students should be informed of the name and telephone number of this person, as well as the established school procedures for informing the media. It is extremely important that the assigned contact person be readily accessible, have good public relations skills, and already have established a positive relationship with the local media.

Before an emergency occurs, school personnel should make every effort to notify the media of positive school events. In a crisis, these professionals will then be more willing to work closely with the school to avoid additional problems.

There have been many horror stories of reporters from newspapers, radio, and television roaming the halls of a school after a suicide, speaking to students while the cameras were grinding, and causing a great deal of grief among the students, faculty, and staff. Although they should already be aware of the possibility, representatives from the media should be advised of the danger of contagion if a suicide is highly publicized or dramatized. Studies have shown that newspaper reports about suicide, as well as television programs and films, are associated with increases in suicide rates, particularly among young people (Bollen & Phillips, 1982; Gould, M.S., & Shaffer, 1986; Phillips & Carstensen, 1986).

Notifying Community Agencies

Representatives from community agencies, previously listed as contacts, should also be notified. Survivors of suicide and other volunteer groups can provide valuable assistance during a suicide crisis. Substitute teachers who are already familiar with the school would also be helpful in an emergency.

Holding a Pre-School Faculty Meeting

A meeting should be scheduled at least an hour before school begins on the next school day to give the faculty time to get ready to meet the students. The school plan, which may call for a temporary change of schedule or student grouping, should be reviewed. The faculty and staff should be given any new information, and the crisis plan should be implemented. The faculty and staff should be informed of the kinds of behaviors and feelings they should expect from the students and themselves. Teachers may also be told exactly what should be said to the students; such instruction provides some measure of security for the teacher and assures that the statements will be consistent throughout the faculty. Mental health professionals should be invited to the meeting to provide information and dispel fear.

Requesting Assistance from Other Schools or Districts

Depending on the size of the school or district, assistance may be needed from surrounding schools or districts. Especially important are additional school psychologists, nurses, social workers, and counselors, who can work with students, staff, or parents.

Informing the Students

It is important to give accurate information to the students, because rumors abound during a suicide crisis. A small group setting is preferable for this discussion; assemblies or large groups should be avoided. A regularly scheduled first-period home room grouping, led by a teacher with whom the students have already established rapport, is most appropriate. The teacher should impart the information simply and accurately. The students should be told that they may ask questions and discuss the matter if they wish. They should also be informed of the school procedures that have been placed in effect, including the establishment of a school crisis center and the availability of counselors and other personnel to assist.

Establishing an In-School Crisis Center

A crisis center, staffed by school counselors, psychologists, nurses, social workers, community mental health professionals, and trained volunteers, can be established in an office or a classroom. Students should be encouraged to come at any time during the day to talk. Peer counselors may be available to patrol the halls and escort troubled students to the crisis center.

Encouraging Students to Express Feelings

Students should be informed that individual reactions to this kind of situation will differ. They may feel sadness, anger, rage, loss, confusion, or fear. They might feel nothing at all.

Students should be encouraged to talk to parents, friends, ministers, teachers, and others about their feelings. They may excuse themselves from class to go to the school crisis center if they wish. They should also support one another and encourage friends who are upset to go to the crisis center. Students need the security of knowing that the adults in their lives have the situation under control.

Notifying Parents of Extremely Affected Students

If any student exhibits an extreme reaction of grief, depression, or suicidal behavior, the parents or guardians must be informed; and the student must be closely supervised until the parent or another adult can assume responsibility. Parents must be made aware of the need for close supervision during a time of crisis.

Grieving students should not be allowed to leave school unless the parents have given permission and a responsible adult will be there. Parents should also be cautioned not to allow students to stay at home because they are upset. School personnel should carefully document the calls to parents, including the date, time, and information given.

Having a Counselor Follow the Victim's Classes

Students who attended class or participated in extracurricular activities with the victim may be in particular need of assistance. A counselor can follow the victim's class and activity schedule and give the students an opportunity to discuss their feelings and to deal with the loss. For example, students may have intense reactions of grief, fear, or uneasiness at the sight of the empty chair in the classroom. A teacher might arrange in advance for a volunteer to occupy the chair or simply have it removed from the classroom.

Students have even had serious reactions to being issued a textbook that had previously been issued to a suicide victim. If the books are to be reused the following term, a wide felt marker might be used to mark out the victim's name, or a new bookplate could be inserted.

Gathering the Belongings of the Deceased

Family survivors of a suicide victim have often told of their devastating feelings of loss because the personal belongings of the suicide victim were not recovered from the school. Such items as athletic equipment, gym clothing, artwork, notebooks, trophies, musical instruments, jackets, books, and papers may be in many locations throughout the school—in lockers, band rooms, exhibits, dressing rooms, or teachers' desks. These articles should be carefully collected and delivered to the principal, who will in turn return them to the family. Further, if the victim had been recently giving away personal possessions, efforts should be made to reclaim these if the family should so desire.

Provision of "Roaming" Substitute Teachers

Faculty should be encouraged to call for assistance if they should be overcome by grief, anxiety, or weariness. Administrators, counselors, and other ancillary personnel from the school or district could be made available to substitute for part of a class period, so that the teacher could rest for a moment and regain composure.

Provision of Counselors for Faculty and Staff

A crisis counselor should also be made available during the day, stationed in the staff lounge or administrator's office, for faculty and staff who may need to discuss their feelings or concerns regarding individual students or the school procedures. Meetings should also be held immediately after school each day for purposes of assessment and further planning. Situations may arise that were not addressed in the school plan, or some part of the plan may not be effective. Records should be kept of any change in procedure and the reasons for the change.

Klagsbrun (cited in Ring, 1984) has noted that a great fear, from an administrator's perspective, is that the reputation of the school will suffer. Administrators also need the follow-up meetings each day to reassure themselves that everything humanly possible is being done to help the students, faculty, and staff.

Holding Evening Parent Meetings—and Student Meetings

Evening meetings should be held for parents and other members of the community who may have questions and concerns. Parents should be encouraged to use the school as a resource if their children exhibit signs of distress. Parents who have been previously unwilling to face the fact that their child may be having problems may come forward and request help for the child during this time.

It is especially important that students who may be seriously affected by the suicide are not left alone. If supervision at home is not available, a meeting for students could be held at the same time as the parent meeting.

Providing Information About Memorial Service or Funeral

It would be preferable, as discussed previously, that the funeral or memorial service be held after school hours or during the weekend, so that the student's suicide does not provide a holiday for the school. The school should provide information to the students regarding the day and time of the services, and students must be responsible for their own transportation. If the funeral occurs during the school day, written permission from a student's family should be required before the student leaves the school.

Visiting the Bereaved Family

The principal and other members of the faculty should visit the family as soon as possible. The visitors can return the student's personal belongings and express the sympathy and concern of the school staff. This would also afford the opportunity to gather information and discuss provisions that might be helpful to surviving siblings or close friends of the victim.

Working with Survivors

A comprehensive suicide prevention program should attend to the needs of survivors—the siblings, family, friends, and adults who were in close contact with the victim. In the case of a student suicide, the entire community, as well as the student body, may be considered to be at risk for some period of time. Over the days, weeks, and months to follow, the school's staff should continue to monitor the behavior of students who show signs of emotional distress and to maintain communication with their parents or guardians. Siblings and close friends, particularly anyone who was romantically involved with the victim, will need special attention. Their grief may be expressed in a variety of ways, including inappropriate behavior, somatic complaints, depression, and learning problems. They will need understanding, encouragement, and support; they also may need some flexibility in assignments and assistance with schoolwork. It is crucial that the teachers and administrators have realistic expectations for the academic performance of grieving students.

School faculty and staff can also be of assistance by putting the victim's family in contact with survivors' self-help groups in the community, such as Compassionate Friends or Survivors of Suicide. Although these groups should not be used as a substitute for counseling or therapy, they may often provide comfort and hope to the family.

MODIFYING THE SCHOOL PLAN

As soon as the crisis is over, the planning committee should meet for the purpose of reviewing the school procedures. In the light of recent events, the committee should make any changes deemed necessary and then resubmit the plan to the faculty and staff for their review.

19. Special Education's Role and Responsibility

Although many suicidal students may not become the responsibility of special education, special education personnel should participate in both the planning and the implementation of the school program for suicide prevention. Special educators, who are not strangers to the problems of suicidal behavior, can be valuable resources within the individual school or district. They have been trained to conduct observations, to assist in the diagnostic process, to work closely with parents, to plan appropriate interventions, and to evaluate outcomes. They usually have established positive relationships with mental health professionals and representatives from other community agencies. They are also attuned to the need for a positive environment, which is a critical component in an effective suicide prevention program. In some communities, the special educator may be the only trained professional available to work with a suicidal child. (One teacher made the comment during a suicide prevention workshop, "In my town, I am Mental Health!")

The advantages of using special education resources in a school suicide prevention program have not gone unnoticed by professionals in the field of mental health. Berkovitz (1985) has listed special education as an important resource for prevention of youth suicide, and a report from the U.S. Department of Health and Human Services states the following:

> Many programs that are not directly aimed at suicide prevention—such as special education programs or family counseling services for adolescents with behavioral problems—may have an effect upon the suicide rate. In any particular location, these indirect programs may be more important than programs designed to prevent suicide. (CDC, 1986)

CRISIS PROCEDURES FOR SPECIAL EDUCATION

The school's suicide prevention plan should be suitable for all students, so that there is no need for a separate crisis procedure for exceptional children. Special education assessment is, however, a valuable procedure to be included in the school suicide prevention plan. If an exceptional child shows signs of suicidal behavior, school personnel should follow the procedures established for the school or district and also report the child's behavior to the special education assessment team. The special education team can convene to discuss appropriate interventions. Special educators should also participate as members of the crisis teams at the school and district levels.

Advantages of Special Education Assessment

Although many suicidal children may not meet the criteria for special education placement, the special education assessment process provides a means of informing and consulting with parents or guardians, which is to the school's advantage as well as the child's. Failure to notify parents of children's suicidal behavior has been cited as a reason for several recent lawsuits against schools in the United States. A comprehensive assessment may also reveal health problems, learning problems, or emotional problems that were previously undetected and that may be related to the child's suicidal behavior.

Minneapolis Public School Plan

The City of Minneapolis Public Schools (1986) have developed exemplary guidelines for suicide prevention in the schools that reflect the collaborative planning of special education, regular education, and community mental health agencies. The guidelines also provide for cooperation of regular and special education in the intervention process, including assessment of a suicidal student for possible services in the program for emotionally or behaviorally disordered students. The guidelines clearly state, however, that special education assessment is not to be used in lieu of immediate parent notification or as the initial step in assessing suicidal risk when more immediate steps are obviously indicated, but rather as an additional resource.

> The E/BD [emotionally/behaviorally disordered] teaming process can be helpful in determining which staff and resources in the building are available to intervene with a student who, while not determined to be immediately at risk, may evidence behaviors that suggest a high-risk profile for suicide. (1986, p. 5)

The Minneapolis guidelines also suggest that, during the assessment process, interventions should be implemented that lessen suicidal risk, such as "parental contact or involvement, use of school staff who offer a safe and supportive environment, and disciplinary approaches that do not increase the student's sense of failure" (p. 5). Another important facet of the Minneapolis plan is the provision of both a building crisis team (within the school) and a citywide crisis support team (at the district level) for purposes of assessing risk, securing parent cooperation, and making decisions for referral and services.

Changes in Special Education Assessment

As previously discussed, authorities have often suggested that evaluation of potential for suicide should be included in the diagnostic procedure for any child who has been referred to a physician or psychiatrist (Pfeffer, 1986). Unless a child has been referred specifically because of suicidal behavior, evaluation of suicidal risk is not normally included in special education assessment, but such evaluation would be a logical addition to the process (see Chapter 14).

Assessment of Adaptive Behavior

Assessment of adaptive behavior, normally included in the diagnosis of mental retardation, should also be included in the evaluation of students who may be suicidal. Adaptive behavior measures would yield valuable information on skills that could be addressed in the Individual Educational Plan (IEP) for exceptional students and in a service plan for students who do not qualify for special education.

Ronald Taylor (1984, 1985) has reviewed the instruments available for measuring adaptive behavior. These instruments provide a structured approach for gathering information in such areas as communication skills, interpersonal relationships, use of leisure time, coping skills, sensory and motor skills, and daily living skills (personal, domestic, and community). As discussed in the section on risk factors, deficits in these skill areas have been found to be related to suicidal behavior in young people.

ASSESSMENT AND PLACEMENT OF DEPRESSED CHILDREN

For several reasons, many depressed or suicidal children are not referred for special education assessment. Although the federal definition of seriously emotionally disturbed in P.L. 94–142 includes a pervasive mood of unhappiness or depression as a characteristic of seriously emotionally disturbed children (Federal Register, 1977), relatively few students meet the other criteria—that the condition exists to a marked degree, that it has existed over an extended period of time, and that it adversely affects educational performance. Problems that are transitory—brought on by situational crises— would not qualify a student for special education. Further, although depression, with its accompanying problems in cognition, would very likely always affect educational performance, students who appear to be functioning satisfactorily (on grade level or above) are rarely brought to the attention of the special education assessment team. A gifted child who is depressed, for example, may appear to be merely unmotivated or disinterested.

Issue of Stigma

A teacher who works with school-aged psychiatric patients has noted that the majority of her suicidal students have been enrolled in regular secondary school prior to hospitalization, and they usually return to the regular school program—not only because they had been making satisfactory progress in school but also because they might suffer from the stigma of being labeled "seriously emotionally disturbed" (Edelman-Faimalie, personal communication, 1986). Assessment teams may often consider that special education placement would be an additional blow to the suicidal student's already lowered self-esteem. There is, however, a critical need for follow-up counseling and other related services for the suicidal student that may not be available in the regular setting. A suicide or suicide attempt may occur when a youngster is discharged from the hospital, attempts to resume normal functioning, and finds the demands of school to be overwhelming.

Provision of Services—Not Necessarily Movement

Parents and school personnel alike should understand that "placement" in special education does not necessarily mean "movement." Eligibility for special education services does not necessarily mean that the student will be moved to another educational setting, but rather that educational and related services will be provided. These services may range from special materials, specialized instruction, or educational counseling within the regular school to the provision of education in a residential setting. Special education can bring a host of ancillary services to bear upon the problems of depressed or suicidal students.

Need for the Full Continuum of Special Education Services

Many depressed or suicidal youth may be functioning well in academics but still be in need of some additional support. An appropriate special education program for such students might be in regular education with an itinerant teacher or teacher consultant—with or without other related services. It is important that the full continuum of special education services is available for such children.

Programming for Depressed Youngsters

As discussed in Chapter 10, some forms of therapy may be too stressful for depressed or suicidal youngsters. Educators must understand that some management procedures may also create additional destructive stress and are therefore dangerous for a depressed or suicidal child. Positive approaches that emphasize encouragement and support are to be preferred to a "get tough" approach—in treatment facilities as well as in school. For example, the father of a young suicide victim suggested that depressed and suicidal residents in halfway houses should be rewarded for progress and not punished for failure:

> Threatening to take away privileges because they aren't looking for work is putting too much pressure on them. Most jobs put pressure on depressed people to do more than they can do in their slowed-down state.

Though this father was not a mental health professional, his perceptions were accurate. Many professionals have stated that the period immediately following release from a hospital or residential setting is a particularly dangerous period for a depressed patient. Failure, fear of failure, or too much pressure from teachers, parents, counselors, or therapists at that time may push a suicidal youngster over the brink. The implications for classroom behavior management systems are obvious; they should provide for positive reinforcement rather than aversive consequences.

IMPLICATIONS OF HANDICAPPING CONDITIONS FOR SUICIDE PREVENTION

Certain handicapping conditions have implications for both curricular modifications and related services for suicidal students. For example, individual or group therapy (which is often suggested as treatment for suicidal youth) might be ineffective with youngsters who have hearing problems or language disorders. Suicidal children who are mentally retarded may need a more directive approach rather than therapy. Learning disabled students, as suggested by Pfeffer (1981), may need therapy for emotional problems as well as a remedial program that addresses areas of academic deficit. Treatment for suicidal behavior, as well as the educational program, must be suited to the child's needs and abilities.

SPECIAL CONSIDERATIONS FOR GIFTED STUDENTS

Gifted students are by no means immune to feelings of low self-worth, depression, and suicidal behavior. Underachieving gifted students, in particular, should be closely monitored for signs of depression or suicidal tendencies. Gifted students who are also handicapped by emotional disturbance, learning disabilities, or physical problems are in particular need of special programs aimed at enhancing socialization, coping skills, and self-esteem.

WORKING WITH SUICIDAL BEHAVIORALLY DISORDERED STUDENTS

An appropriate instructional program for a behaviorally disordered child is an important facet of a suicide prevention plan. Because the major presenting problems of a behaviorally disordered child lie in the social and affective domains, the IEP for such a student should always reflect assessment and instruction in this area. "Affective education is not an extra. It is an essential component of special education as it is formulated under the mandate of Public Law 94–142" (Morse, Ardizzone, MacDonald, & Pasick, 1980). The specific factors that may be contributing to the suicidal behavior of an individual child should also be addressed in both the educational program and the provision of related services.

Provision of Therapy or Counseling

For a child who has been identified as seriously emotionally disturbed, counseling and therapy can be made available as related services. Funding for these services, however, generally presents a problem. A perusal of the IEPs of 10 suicidal students who were identified as "severely emotionally disturbed" revealed no reference to suicide or to the provision of therapy. Special education assessment teams may often be reluctant to suggest counseling or therapy, particularly on a long-term basis, because of the expense to the school program.

Therapy is not normally provided as part of the educational program for children who have not been diagnosed as seriously emotionally disturbed. If a suicidal child is already receiving special education for any other handicapping condition, referral for reassessment may be advisable.

Need for Case Management

An additional problem related to suicide prevention with behaviorally disordered students is that they may often be served by a variety of agencies with very little coordination of efforts. These children may be clients of a number of community agencies (e.g., departments of law enforcement, social services, education, mental health, and vocational rehabilitation) that may not be collaborating in a treatment plan. There is a critical need for case management for these children, so that they do not either "fall through the cracks" or have several simultaneous treatment plans that work at cross purposes.

Talking About Suicide

If information about suicide (e.g., warning signs, referral procedures, available resources) is to be related directly to behaviorally disordered students, special procedures may be indicated. Behaviorally disordered students may often react poorly to discussions of suicide, particularly if the group leader is not someone with whom they have already established a positive relationship.

An outreach counselor from a local hospital, who had been offering suicide prevention information to the normal high school population, came to the resource room for emotionally disturbed students to conduct a similar session. The students, the majority of whom were or had been suicidal, reacted very poorly to the discussion. Some were visibly upset and one pulled his jacket up over his head throughout the period. After the psychologist left, I asked the students for explanations of their behavior. They answered that they didn't want to talk about suicide. Their comments included, "Talking about it makes me feel worse," and "It reminds me of all the times I've screwed up." (McGee, personal communication, 1985)

Concept of Neutralization

Jacobson and Faegre (1969) proposed the control of instructional materials and procedures in the classroom for disturbed children so that the materials do not contribute to additional anxiety. This technique is particularly valuable in teaching a suicidal child.

Classroom material should be screened for classroom use; if it appears to have a high potential for upsetting a student, it is simply replaced by more neutral material. If potential dangers are apparent in only a small section or passage, the teacher should be prepared to neutralize it by explanation—in a calm and matter-of-fact manner.

> "Casual," "gentle," "matter-of-fact," "self-assured"—these are keys to on-the-spot neutralization of a touchy issue. If the teacher is uncomfortable about a question, if he implies blame or ridicule, if he shows curiousity about the child's feelings, he risks increasing the child's anxiety and inner agitation. (Jacobson & Faegre, 1969, p. 253)

Importance of the School Environment

Maris (1981) found that negative interaction (hostile, rejecting relationships) related positively to dissatisfaction, hopelessness, and suicide in his study. According to Maris, negative interaction is a more important factor in both suicides and suicide attempts than is social isolation. He has suggested that suicide prevention workers should not assume that suicidal people have no significant others; they need to concentrate instead on the quality of the suicidal individual's social interaction with significant others.

Negative interaction has often been observed in the families of suicidal children and youth, but it also occurs in the school. By definition, seriously emotionally disturbed children exhibit the inability to build and maintain satisfactory interpersonal relationships. Educational programs for behaviorally disordered children should therefore always focus on the enhancement of appropriate social interaction. Classrooms must be structured so that behaviorally disordered students interact with one another in a positive way. Behaviorally disordered students (especially those who are suicidal) must not be subjected to threats, scapegoating, or ridicule—either from fellow students or from adults in the school environment. A major responsibility of special educators is to provide a positive environment for exceptional students. The importance of this one factor cannot be overemphasized; it is a critical issue in suicide prevention.

Need for a Positive Approach

Many suicide prevention workers have emphasized the necessity to maintain a positive, upbeat, and confident manner with suicidal individuals. It is important for teachers, as well as therapists, to understand that many suicidal individuals have frequent suicidal thoughts that they cannot control. An appropriate approach for such students might be bombardment with positive input, which might make it difficult for them to think about anything depressing (for at least the time that they are in school).

Working with Parents of Behaviorally Disordered Students

Maintaining communication with the parents or guardians of any depressed or suicidal child is extremely important; in the case of a suicidal behaviorally disordered child it is crucial. Many behaviorally disordered students have a history of family problems, and the parents or guardians may often feel weary, helpless, and hopeless themselves. The parents of these children are in great need of communication, direction, and emotional support.

SPECIAL CONSIDERATIONS FOR ABUSED HANDICAPPED CHILDREN

If there are indications of abuse, as previously discussed, the parents may not be the first to be notified when a student is verbalizing intent to commit suicide. The problem is instead reported to the appropriate child protection agency. Such a decision should not be made by a single teacher or counselor; the school or district crisis team should assist in making such a decision and should carefully document (in writing) the situation, agency to which the incident was reported, means of reporting, date, and time.

> At a workshop for school personnel, a young high school teacher (who had grown up in that school district) shared the following comments, "If anybody from the school had called my parents and told them that I was suicidal, suicide wouldn't have been a problem. They would have killed me themselves."
> This young teacher had been suicidal during her high school years as a result of severe physical abuse by both of her parents. She had left home at her earliest opportunity. Her handicapped sister, who had also been abused but who had to remain at home, had recently committed suicide. She warned that school authorities should be extremely careful about notifying parents of a student's suicidal behavior and should never do so without first discussing this action with the student.

Abuse of handicapped children and adolescents (in the home or at school) is not uncommon ("Child Abuse," 1987). Teachers, counselors, social workers, and other educational personnel must be knowledgeable about the symptoms of abuse, the laws of the state or province regarding the reporting of abuse, and the appropriate legal procedures to follow. Law enforcement agents, attorneys, and judges should also become informed about the special considerations necessary for determining abuse in handicapped children, particularly in those who may be nonverbal and therefore unable to report maltreatment or testify in their own behalf.

FAMILY SERVICES: A NEW FRONTIER

Although special education professionals have been working closely with parents for many years, the focus has often been on advising them, rather than working with them as equals or considering their needs or preferences in determining an appropriate educational program. Materials have recently been developed that are designed for purposes of determining and meeting family needs as well as facilitating family participation in formulating the child's IEP. These materials would seem to be particularly useful in working with the parents of a suicidal exceptional child.

Dr. Lisbeth Vincent of the University of Wisconsin and her colleagues (Vincent, Davis, Brown, Miller, & Gruenewald, 1983) have developed a checklist system to help parents of handicapped children identify skills that their children can already perform, skills that are unimportant to parents, and skills that the parents want their children to learn. Parents also record the child's activities, their own activities, and those of other family members in intervals for 3- to 5-day time periods. This information is then used in IEP meetings as a way of determining goals for the child.

Wilcox and Bellamy (1987) have developed an activity catalogue to facilitate collaboration between parents and professionals. Families use *The Catalogue* to select activities, such as attending a movie, going shopping, or balancing a checkbook, in which they would like their children to participate ("Family Services," 1986). Parents and professionals together negotiate activities to be included in the child's IEP.

As mentioned in the next chapter—on primary prevention— establishing links between and among the child's several "worlds" is an important facet of an effective suicide prevention program. Procedures and materials that enhance this effort, such as those previously discussed, are particularly important for the suicidal handicapped child.

20. Primary Prevention in the Schools: Enhancing Emotional Health

In addition to procedures to follow in the aftermath of suicide (postvention), and procedures for the detection and referral of depressed and suicidal students and the provision of services in the school and community (intervention), an effective school program will include measures for the primary prevention of youth suicide. Problems that may put children and adolescents at risk for serious emotional problems should be addressed before the onset of suicidal behavior.

Many of the risk factors associated with suicidal behavior in children and youth cannot be changed, such as a family history of suicide, depression, or mental illness; a family history of divorce, separation, and loss; or a personal history of illness or handicapping condition. Other risk factors are beyond the control of the school, such as incarceration, child abuse, publicity about suicide, or the availability of weapons.

Educators clearly understand that the school's efforts should be focused on alterable variables, rather than on problems that are beyond its jurisdiction (Bloom, 1980). Fortunately, studies have shown that the school can exert considerable influence on variables that were once considered to be unalterable, such as the effects of family background or parental neglect (Joyce & Showers, 1987).

IMPLEMENTING LONG-TERM STRATEGIES

As previously mentioned, sufficient and effective psychological services should be provided so that counseling is quickly available in the school, and students should be encouraged to use these resources. Counselors, social workers, psychologists, school nurses, and school resource officers should be considered as integral members of the faculty and staff and should participate in regular school activities and extracurricular events.

Pocket-sized "help cards," on which are printed the telephone numbers and addresses of community resources (e.g., abuse registry, family service center, rape crisis center, Alanon, Alateen, runaway hotline, emergency mental health services, emergency medical services, fire department, law enforcement) can be distributed to all students, faculty, and staff. If there is a community crisis center or hotline, a poster that highlights its telephone number can be displayed in each classroom. Community businesses and organizations may be persuaded to underwrite the costs of these materials.

A buddy system for new students and their families, similar to the "welcome wagon" for new neighbors, can be established. Orientation programs can be conducted throughout the year and peer counselors can be made available to ameliorate the problems related to being in an unfamiliar environment.

The school counselor can hold regularly scheduled group discussions that focus on common problems. Peer counselors, under supervision, can act as facilitators in these groups.

Instructional Units on Suicide Prevention

Many schools provide a unit or component on suicide prevention as part of an existing course. This unit may often be included in health education, home economics, or a similar course required of all students. Any course that deals with life management skills or emotional health is an appropriate place. In some schools, the material is presented by the school counselor, nurse, social worker, or psychologist; in others, the regular classroom teacher is responsible for the presentation.

Procedures for Presentation to Students

Ideally, suicide prevention information would be presented in small groups (by an individual who already knows the students), so that the students' responses could be carefully monitored. A rule of thumb is simply "the smaller the group the better."

The least problematical approach in the classroom (with the lowest potential for creating additional problems) is that of simple discussion, preferably led by a teacher or staff member whom the students already know and trust. The discussion should focus on (a) resources (including the school) available to provide assistance for students in need, and (b) steps young people can take to help themselves, their friends, and their family. The information given to students should be simple, factual, and practical.

As discussed in Chapter 3, the question of whether classroom discussion can trigger suicidal thoughts and actions is still unresolved. The emphasis in classroom discussion, therefore, should be on solving problems rather than dwelling on them, on emotional health rather than mental illness, and on living rather than dying.

The Florida training manual (State of Florida, 1987) includes materials suitable for the secondary classroom and guidelines for the person responsible for presenting these materials. The student materials emphasize emotional and physical health, stressing positive ways to cope with problems. The word "suicide" does not appear in these materials; the terms used instead are "emotional distress" or "self-destructive behavior." The unit can be covered in approximately 150 minutes and is intended for use as part of a mental health unit in the Life Skills course required for high school graduation. The topics, which are presented in classroom discussion and handouts, include (a) learning to cope with life's problems, (b) communicating and sharing problems, (c) things you can do to help yourself, (d) helping a friend in crisis, (e) developing healthy attitudes, (f) coping skills, and (g) reducing self-generated stress.

A Caveat About Instructional Materials

The use of films, videos, and audiotapes in a suicide prevention program is not recommended. Films and videos are used in the classroom precisely because they make the material more attractive and exciting, because they have a greater emotional impact than simple discussion. It is inadvisable to make information about suicide more attractive or exciting. Nothing should be said or done in the classroom that makes suicidal behavior appear to be acceptable.

Some of the earlier school programs aimed at suicide prevention contained material and activities that would now be considered objectionable. For example, several programs included a survey on students' attitudes toward death—an instrument developed by trained mental health professionals for use with adults who might work with suicidal youth. It was not intended for use with students. Programs in place for several years should be reexamined with regard to both the content of the material presented and the methods used in presenting that material.

Particularly distasteful and potentially harmful are such classroom activities as having students write their own epitaphs or plan their own funerals. In one case (cited in Schlafly, 1985), a teenager shot herself to death after writing a note on her front door stating what she would like to have inscribed on her tombstone. This activity had been included in a unit on death in a school English class.

According to several researchers, some suicide prevention programs do little to change participants' attitudes about suicide, and some may even have a negative impact on those most in need of help. Shaffer (cited in Viadero, 1987) has suggested that didactic approaches may upset students who are predisposed to suicide. Shaffer and Garland (cited in Viadero, 1987) have been conducting a study in 11 New Jersey high schools, 6 of which have state-funded suicide prevention programs and 5 of which do not. They found that the vast majority of students in all of the schools (with or without the program) already had what the researchers consider to be desirable attitudes toward suicide—that suicide is not a good solution, that suicide threats should always be taken seriously, and that a friend's intention to kill himself should not be kept secret. The researchers also found that the proportion of students with those attitudes was almost the same before and one month after the school programs. Students who admitted to having had suicidal thoughts described the programs as "upsetting" or "boring" and as making their own problems "more difficult to handle" (Viadero, 1987, p. 7). David Phillips, who has studied suicide contagion, offered the following comment on these findings: "In America, we have this wonderfully naive belief that all that's necessary to cure something is a program . . . . It doesn't occur to us that we may have a negative effect or no effect at all" (Viadero, 1987, p. 7).

A Preventive Curriculum

Special courses or special topics within existing courses may assist youngsters in learning to cope with common problems and can therefore be considered as a preventive curriculum. Such courses or topics include

- Basic skills (for those who need remedial work.
- Stress reduction (time management, organizational skills, relaxation training).
- Coping skills.
- Problem solving.
- Decision making.
- Self-control.
- Assertiveness training.
- "Outlets" (art, music, dance, drama).

- Prescriptive physical education (weight training, weight loss, body building, exercise).
- Individual "life" sports (tennis, racquetball, handball, golf, running).
- Adolescent health problems (nutrition, hygiene, skin care, orthodontics, optometry).
- Grooming and dress (clothing selection, color analysis, cosmetics).
- Group discussion and problem resolution.
- Communication skills.
- Juvenile law.
- Career and vocational education.
- Marriage and family living.
- Use of leisure time (hobbies, community service, creative writing, recreational reading).
- Drug education.
- Sex education (Guetzloe, 1987).

This is by no means an exhaustive list. Any topic that emphasizes a positive approach to managing problems would be appropriate for inclusion somewhere in the regular school curriculum.

MEETING CHILDREN'S BASIC NEEDS

Several authorities have suggested that there are certain basic needs that must be met by all human beings, and that these needs are either hierarchical or developmental. Maslow (1954, 1962) has proposed such a hierarchy, including (in the following order): physiological needs; safety and security; belonging, affection, and love; respect for others; self-respect; and self-actualization. According to Maslow, lower level needs must be met before an individual can respond to needs at the higher levels.

As mentioned earlier, mental health professionals have suggested that the school curriculum should be more relevant to the developmental tasks of its students, particularly at the adolescent level (Berkovitz, 1985; Freud, cited in Shneidman, 1969). Havighurst (1952) has proposed that certain tasks must be accomplished specifically at the adolescent stage of development. They include the following:

1. Achieving new and more mature relationsips with peers of both sexes.

2. Achieving a masculine or feminine social role.
3. Accepting one's physique and using the body effectively.
4. Achieving emotional independence of parents and other adults.
5. Achieving assurance of economic independence.
6. Selecting and preparing for an occupation.
7. Preparing for marriage and family life.
8. Developing intellectual skills and concepts necessary for civic competence.
9. Desiring and achieving socially responsible behavior.
10. Acquiring a set of values and an ethical system as a guide to behavior (Havighurst, 1952).

Development of a Sense of Self-Preservation

Another perspective on the basic needs of children is related to the child's development of a sense of self-preservation. Psychoanalysts have proposed that a suicidal child has "personality vulnerabilities" (Pfeffer, 1986, p. 45) that evolve as a result of interaction between constitutional factors, developmental processes, and early life experiences. A child develops a sense of self-preservation through interaction with important people in the environment.

According to Khantzian and Mack (1983), the following functions must be developed for adequate self-preservation: (a) sufficient self-esteem to feel worth protecting; (b) the capacity to understand situations of risk; (c) ability to control impulses; (d) pleasure in mastering situations of risk; (e) enough knowledge about the outside world to survive in it; (f) ability to be assertive for purposes of self-protection; and (g) the ability to choose companions that will enhance, rather than jeopardize, one's protection. Pfeffer (1986) has listed the following factors that the environment must provide if a child is to develop a healthy sense of self-preservation:

1. Protection of the child from injury.
2. Structure, so that the child knows what to expect.
3. Opportunity to play and explore.
4. Freedom to express emotions without being punished.

These functions could be taught and the environmental factors could be provided in a school program designed for the prevention of self-destructive behavior.

Development of Self-Esteem

The importance of low self-esteem as a factor related to suicidal behavior has been emphasized by many mental health professionals and educators. Self-esteem is a personal judgment that indicates the extent to which the individual believes himself to be powerful, worthy, competent, and significant (Coopersmith, 1967).

Coopersmith (1967), in a study of the antecedents of self-esteem, found that individuals come to evaluate themselves on the bases of (a) how well they can influence and control others (power); (b) how well they meet moral and ethical standards (virtue or worthiness); (c) how proficient they are in performing tasks and meeting standards for achievement (competence); and (d) the degree to which they gain attention, acceptance, and affection from others (significance). Coopersmith further found that young people viewed significance and competence as more important than worthiness and power. Some of Coopersmith's other findings that have obvious implications for school programs are the following:

1. *The importance of self-awareness and self-evaluation.* An individual might attain success in an area that he does not regard as important, such as competence, and conclude that he is unworthy because he has not succeeded by the criterion he values most, such as virtue. Determining the bases that a given individual uses in judging his own worth may be a crucial first step in determining the source of his difficulties and in guiding therapeutic efforts (Coopersmith, 1967).

2. *Discipline practices that result in low self-esteem.* Dominating discipline practices tend to result in lowered self-esteem (Coopersmith, 1967). Parents of children with low self-esteem are themselves low in self-esteem. They lack the confidence necessary to establish a family framework, and they rely on harsh treatment to exercise control over their children.

3. *Discipline practices that result in high self-esteem.* Limits for children with high self-esteem are generally well-defined and enforced, but not harsh or unduly restrictive. Mothers of children with high self-esteem are most likely to employ management procedures such as reward, restraint, denial, or separation and are least likely to use corporal punishment and withdrawal of affection. Parental respect for children is manifested by efforts to clarify and justify policies, willingness to allow free expression of opinion, and encouragement of participation in planning and decision making.

4. *The need for limits and structure.* The conditions for learning positive self-attitudes generally are more structured, specific, and demanding than the traditional therapeutic setting. There is a need, according to Coopersmith (1967), for clearly defined rules and limits enforced by reasonable people.

According to Jones (1980), schools and other institutions should examine their environments to determine whether they are meeting basic needs and providing for the development of positive self-esteem. He has suggested that schools should attend to such basic needs as physical comfort, flexibility in scheduling when students are ill or fatigued, attention to pace and scheduling of daily activities, and concern for physical safety. Schools should also provide psychological security, reduce the number of anxiety-provoking evaluations, and increase the number of positive statements regarding student worth. Jones has developed strategies for teaching and counseling adolescents that are based on both the developmental tasks of adolescents (Havighurst, 1952) and Coopersmith's (1967) findings on self-esteem.

Preventing Damage to a Child's Self-Esteem

Williams (1984) has described events that lower self-esteem in children, including difficulty in mixing with other children, being bullied over an extended period, feeling different from the peer group, feeling unwanted, and feeling hated. Such situations abound in the school.

Many adults can still remember too well the humiliation they suffered in school at the hands of students or teachers. One individual, who had been an awkward child, commented that he still feels the pain of being always the last child chosen by his peers for a team.

> The unfortunate truth is that many conditions that create stress and depression in students are directly related to school events. The nation's movement toward "academic excellence," which will result in failure, exclusion, and second class citizenship for many students, may prove to be a contributing factor. Many reports of suicide have cited school problems as precipitating events. The school itself may be causing the deaths of many of the nation's young. (Guetzloe, 1987, p. 3)

Every rule and procedure in the classroom or school should be examined with reference to its possible effect on a child's sense of self-worth. School procedures that cause damage to children should not be tolerated.

ENHANCING SELF-ESTEEM IN THE SCHOOL

A school-aged child's competence is generally measured—by himself and others—in terms of his ability to function in the school setting. The school can take steps toward enhancing self-esteem by simply teaching the basic skills that enable a child to be successful in the school environment, but self-esteem can also be addressed directly in the school curriculum.

Materials for Teaching Self-Esteem

Reasoner (1982) has developed a teacher's guide and classroom materials based on Coopersmith's (1967) study of self-esteem. Included in this program are guidelines for establishing a school environment that should foster a sense of security, a sense of identity, a sense of belonging, a sense of purpose, and a sense of personal competence, characteristics associated with self-esteem and motivation. The program is the culmination of 10 years of research and experimentation and has been evaluated as highly successful (Reasoner, 1982).

Need for Effective Models

Coopersmith (1967) has suggested that a student with low self-esteem may benefit by modeling the behavior of an effective, assured, and competent individual, learning how such a person deals with anxiety, makes decisions, deals with failures and insults, and makes friends. The child may model alternative ways of working with people that result in a greater sense of power and control. According to Coopersmith, the style of response may be even more important than the specific action.

Modeling Self-Esteem and Social Fidelity

Erikson (1964) noted two important sources of weakness related to emotional health in adolescents—the lack of self-esteem and the lack of social fidelity. In a discussion of youth suicide, Havighurst (1969) blamed society for compounding the problems of young people by making their choices of a career more complicated, forcing them to be socially precocious, and exposing them to the "seamy side of personal and political life" (p. 65). Adolescents are confronted with the tasks of performing in school, choosing an occupation, and establishing relationships with the opposite sex at an earlier age than were adolescents of several generations ago. The school should assist adolescents in developing both confidence in themselves and commitment to society by providing the following elements in the school program:

1. Opportunity for service to the school, the community, and society—a variety of projects during both the academic year and the summer. A current good example would be the Habitat for

Humanity program, which assists in providing housing for families with low incomes.

2. Curriculum that places emphasis on the achievements of modern society in solving problems of educational and economic opportunity, public health, and poverty.

3. Teachers who are good models of both self-esteem and social fidelity, who are oriented toward improving society and making positive contributions to others (Havighurst, 1969).

Importance of Supportive Relationships with Adults

Shrier (Shrier & Johnson, 1985) has suggested that several factors have contributed to the significant increase in suicide among young people over the past two decades.

Adolescence is a vulnerable stage in the life cycle due to the variety of physical, cognitive, and psychosocial changes involved; societal changes in the direction of increased alienation, isolation, and weakened family and community supports; and specific individual and familial risk factors affecting important relationships during the preadolescent years. (Shrier & Johnson, 1985, p. 74)

According to Shrier (Shrier & Johnson, 1985), adolescents can learn to cope with life's stresses in the context of consistent, reliable, and caring relationships with adults. She has suggested the development of school and community programs aimed at increasing a sense of competence and establishing supportive relationships with adults who can serve as appropriate role models.

Outcomes of Supportive Relationships—Resilient Children

For a number of years, psychologists and psychiatrists have been studying the characteristics of children who seem to thrive despite being brought up in the most chaotic, abusive, or impoverished environments. These children have been labeled "resilient children" or "invulnerable children" by researchers (Anthony & Cohler, 1987; Elkind, 1981; Werner & Smith, 1982). They seem to be endowed with innate characteristics that somehow insulate them from turmoil and pain and that enable them to reach out to some adult—a family member, teacher, or friend—who can lend crucial emotional support. At a very early age, resilient children, despite abuse and neglect, exhibit a high degree of independence, enthusiasm, compliance, and tolerance for frustration. They also show a clear ability to seek help from adults.

Some of the most recent information on the attributes of resilient children came from a study of nearly 700 children born in 1955 on the Hawaiian island of Kauai. All the children were born to impoverished families and were subjected to a number of problems, such as birth trauma or parents who were alcoholic or mentally ill. Over the years, many children showed signs of psychological disturbance, but approximately 10% not only survived the difficulties but also seemed to thrive. Emmy Werner of the University of California at Davis, who is directing the study, interviewed these individuals when they were 30 years of age and found that an important factor related to their success was their ability to find someone who could help them believe that they could succeed. In many cases it was a teacher, from as early as the first grade, who acted as a mentor. Without exception, all the children who thrived had at least one person that provided them consistent emotional support—a grandmother, an older sister, a teacher, or a neighbor. In addition to sociability, which seemed to draw people to them, these children also had an area of special talent or interest that kept them absorbed and that gave them a feeling of confidence.

Educators can learn from these resilient children. While the children's characteristics appeared to be innate, some of these skills can be learned. Mentoring, a technique that often has been used with gifted and other exceptional children, would be a valuable technique for providing appropriate adult models for children at risk for depression, suicidal behavior, or other emotional problems. Instruction in the area of social skills (particularly help-seeking) is also important. Further, providing opportunities for troubled children to enhance their individual areas of creativity and talent might prove to be a valuable intervention (Guetzloe, 1987; Guetzloe & Johnson, 1985).

COMBATTING ALIENATION: ESTABLISHING LINKS

Bronfenbrenner, in a discussion of adolescent alienation, has stressed the importance of establishing links between and among the "four worlds of childhood"—family, peers, school, and work (1986, p. 430). "If the essence of alienation is disconnectedness, then the best way to counteract alienation is through the creation of connecting links" (p. 434). He has suggested that caring should become an essential part of the curriculum, and that children should be asked to "spend time with and to care for younger children, the elderly, the sick, and the lonely . . . . Just as many schools now train superb drum corps, they could also train 'caring corps'—groups of young men and women who would be on call to handle a variety of emergencies" (p. 435). Bronfenbrenner has also agreed that schools should provide mentors—significant and committed adults—for children.

Understanding the Interdependence of Human Beings

In recent years, many adults have lamented that young people have become lost in themselves and interested only in satisfying their own needs, losing sight of their kinship with others. School programs can help to reverse that trend by emphasizing togetherness and by promoting the school as a caring community that brings children together (Luty, 1985).

Links with Peers

Several authorities have made other practical suggestions for establishing links between the child and his peers in the school setting. Crain, Mahard, and Narot (1982), for example, have suggested the creation of long-term subgroups or clusters within large schools—to give students a sense of belonging and being known. Glasser (1986) has suggested the formation of learning teams within the classroom, so that students can practice cooperation. In Plano, Texas, a SWAT (Students Working All Together) team was formed to welcome new students and to get them involved in school activities (Guinn, 1989). This was so successful that several other support groups for students and their families have been established.

Curriculum for Combatting Alienation

The Quest National Center in Columbus, Ohio, in cooperation with Lions Clubs International, has developed a program called Skills for Adolescence, which deals with a wide range of factors commonly associated with alienation (Gerler, 1986). The program, designed to be covered in one semester, is based on a multimodal approach proposed by Lazarus (1978). The materials include units of instruction with detailed lesson plans, a textbook for students, a parent guide, and guidelines for parent seminars. The program has generated considerable enthusiasm among educators and has been adopted by more than 500 school districts in North America (Gerler, 1986).

Links with the Community—A Year-Round School

In the state of New York, an experimental year-round school program is being prepared. It is considered by some to be a modest beginning, but it holds promise for giving disadvantaged children a fair chance to become self-sufficient, contributing citizens. Ten elementary schools in poor neighborhoods will be operated year-round, 7 days a week, from early morning into the evening. They will offer the children an array of special services such as tutoring, weekend activities, and recreation. The extended school day would allow time for students to be immersed in basic skills and would enable working parents to become more involved in school activities. Teams of mentors would be recruited in the community. Retired people, college students, and high school students would tutor and encourage laggard children. Businesses would be encouraged to sponsor a school or send in a team of executives to work with the children. School officials hope that, instead of turning off children already at risk for failure, the program will bring into the social mainstream thousands of deprived children who would otherwise grow up uneducated, unskilled, and unable to participate constructively in American life ("Schools," 1987).

Long-Term Alliances Between Schools and Parents

The need for a system of communication between the school and home was discussed earlier in this text. Cooperation between the school and the family, however, should go far beyond mere communication. Comer (cited in Shrier & Johnson, 1985) has suggested that professionals need to encourage institutional changes that reestablish a sense of community and interaction between and among authority figures in a less authoritarian way than in the past. He has discussed the critical need for positive relationships between and among all of the adults in a child's life.

As an example of positive interaction between parents and schools, Comer (cited in Shrier & Johnson, 1985) has described a program that he established in two inner-city schools in New Haven, Connecticut. In these schools, students' problems of poor attendance, disruptive behavior, and academic deficiencies were reversed through the establishment of a management system that involved parents, teachers, and administrators. These links restored trust between the family and the school.

Parental Involvement in the School Program

Bradshaw (cited in "Parental Involvement," 1987), has proposed that schools accept the responsibility for developing meaningful vehicles for parental participation in the school setting. She has also suggested that employers should be encouraged to give parents time off from work to attend school functions.

Walberg (1984) has also pointed to the importance of family involvement with the school program. Williams (cited in Walberg,

1984) has suggested the following ways in which family members can participate: (a) as an audience for the child (e.g., listening to the child as he reads aloud), (b) as co-learners (e.g., learning computer programming, looking for certain newspaper topics, or watching selected television programs with the child), (c) as supporters of school programs, (d) as advocates for the school before the school board or community officials, (e) as members of school committees, or (f) as paid school employees.

PROGRAMS FOR YOUNG CHILDREN: THE NEED FOR A POSITIVE APPROACH

Many educators have commented on the critical need for programs for young children aimed at both preventing suicide and promoting emotional health. They have expressed the fear that establishing prevention programs at only the high school level may very likely be a case of "locking the barn door after the horse is stolen." As discussed earlier in this text, depression and suicidal behavior have been noted even in children of preschool age.

Parents, however, have expressed concern that suicide prevention programs that focus on death and dying may have adverse effects upon young children (Dickert, personal communication, 1985; Schlafly, 1985). Prevention programs for young children should focus on the enhancement of physical and emotional health, rather than on "gloom and doom." Topics that create fear or feelings of depression in children should be omitted from the curriculum. School should be the place where children would like to be.

Shedlin (1986) has pointed out that between nursery school and sixth grade a child spends 9,000 hours in school—more than twice the amount of time spent in high school. He has proposed a qualitative approach for professionals to use in evaluating an elementary school, using questions such as the following:

1. Do the children and adults seem happy in the school environment?
2. Is there a sense of delight, of enthusiasm and energy, of joy in learning and teaching?
3. Are differences in children's learning styles, developmental levels, and interests celebrated?
4. Is there evidence—in both verbal and nonverbal interactions —that students and adults within the school have mutual regard and respect for one another?
5. Is there evidence that the processes of learning, as well as the outcomes, are valued?

6. Is there time in a child's schedule for relaxation, for imaginative activities, and for pondering?
7. Is there as much interest in the "how" as there is in the "how well?" (Shedlin, 1986)

Although Shedlin (1986) has proposed these questions (and many others) for the assessment of elementary schools, the emphasis on school climate is pertinent for middle schools and high schools as well. The provision of a positive school environment is critical to the success of a program for suicide prevention.

PROVISION OF AN INDIVIDUALIZED PREVENTIVE CURRICULUM

Any inclusion to a student's program that serves to enhance feelings of self-worth, security, or self-control also has the potential for preventing suicidal behavior. Many programs aimed primarily at preventing other serious problems (such as teenage pregnancy, school dropout, or substance abuse) can also be regarded as suicide prevention activities.

The problems of an individual child (or an entire class) can be addressed in a positive way by using the simple "If . . . then" approach described earlier in this text. If a student suffers from unrealistic expectations or overprogramming, then goal-setting, self-evaluation, and self-monitoring would be valuable individual study topics. If social isolation is a problem, then training in assertiveness, communication, and social skills would be advisable. Problems of stress could be addressed by teaching self-control, coping skills, problem-solving, time management, and relaxation exercises. Preparation for the future could be taught in such topics as career and vocational education, government and law, home economics, marriage and family living, and use of leisure time. Problems of low self-esteem can be addressed through instruction in art, music, dance, hygiene, cosmetology, clothing selection, weight training, and individual sports.

Some factors related to youth suicide have already been addressed in instructional materials or guidelines, such as those developed for building self-esteem (Canfield & Wells, 1976; Reasoner, 1982), combatting alienation (Bronfenbrenner, 1986; Gerler, 1986), or teaching self-control (Fagen, Long, & Stevens, 1975). Other variables that are currently under investigation may also have implications for school programs, such as the effects of color, full spectrum light, exercise, role-playing, altruism, and "reality processing" on the emotions of young people (Guetzloe & Rhodes, 1986, 1988; Rhodes & Guetzloe, 1987). Any positive approach that is also "school-friendly" should be explored.

In conclusion, some of the risk factors associated with youth suicide are immutable; history cannot be changed. There is evidence, however, that some variables that were once thought to be unalterable can be changed through appropriate interventions. Many of the risk factors associated with youth suicide can be addressed directly (and successfully) in the school.

21. Epilogue: A Note from the Author

It is an unfortunate sign of the times that there was ever a necessity for any book on youth suicide; but the need has been, and continues to be, apparent. The problem is even more evident than it was when this book was begun. Further, during the time that I chained myself (figuratively speaking) to the typewriter or the computer, it was a rare day on which I did not receive a call or letter from someone who needed information about youth suicide, with the requests coming from many different individuals and agencies—suicidal youngsters and adults, parents, teachers, crisis counselors, newspaper and television reporters, school administrators, representatives from community agencies, students seeking help with papers, fellow authors in search of references, editors and publishers wanting more books and articles, and others too numerous to recount. As I began this section, only a few moments ago, a call came from a high school requesting information and assistance, because a young girl had hanged herself and the entire school was in crisis. Neither the school nor the district had formulated a plan for dealing with this problem.

SO MUCH TO SAY—SO LITTLE TIME

There is so much information that might be helpful to school personnel involved in the prevention of youth suicide that a thousand books would probably not be superfluous; and if I had included only a few words on each available reference, this book would never have been finished. A multitude of books and articles on this topic contain information that would be valuable to a student of suicidology. This text has focused on information that would be useful to teachers and other school personnel in both understanding the problem of youth suicide and in making appropriate decisions regarding interventions within the school.

Further, as mentioned in the first chapter, probably more important than the information that is included in this text is the information that is not. There are many publications—articles, pamphlets, books, and films (some of which are intended for use with children)—that propose interventions that may be dangerous. It is important for those who work with young people, especially in the schools, to follow a cautious and positive approach in developing a prevention program.

Many people, including authorities on suicide, believe—and propose—that the schools should do far more than what has been suggested in this text. The school, however, is only one of the several worlds in which the child lives and learns. The other worlds—the home, peer group, and community—also have responsibilities in this regard. A problem of this magnitude, a matter of life and death, calls for the cooperation of all people who come in contact with children and youth. Youth suicide is everyone's problem and everyone's responsibility.

It is my sincere hope that, in my lifetime, the tragedy of youth suicide will be of only historical interest. I look forward to the day when this book is not only obsolete, but unnecessary. For the time being, I hope that it will be useful.

References

Abram, H. S., Moore, G. L., & Westerfelt, F. B. (1971). Suicidal behavior in chronic dialysis patients. *American Journal of Psychiatry, 127,* 1199–1204.

Accidents, violence tied to youth deaths. (1987, June 26). *St. Petersburg Times,* p. 3A.

Ackerly, W. C. (1967). Latency age children who threaten or attempt to kill themselves. *Journal of the American Academy of Child Psychiatry, 6,* 242–261.

Adams-Tucker, C. (1982). Proximate effects of sexual abuse in childhood: A report in 28 children. *American Journal of Psychiatry, 139,* 1252–1256.

AIDS suicides reported. (1987, August 13). *St. Petersburg Times,* p. 3A.

Allen, N. (1977). History and background of suicidology. In C. L. Hatton, S. M. Valente, & A. Rink (Eds.), *Suicide: Assessment and intervention* (pp. 1–19). New York: Appleton-Century-Crofts.

Alvarez, A. (1972). *The savage god: A study of suicide.* New York: Random House.

Alvarez, A. (1975). Literature in the nineteenth and twentieth centuries. In S. Perlin (Ed.), *A handbook for the study of suicide* (pp. 31–60). New York: Oxford University Press.

American Association of Suicidology. (1977). *Suicide and how to prevent it.* West Point, PA: Merck, Sharp, & Dohme.

American Mental Health Fund (1986). *All he needs is a good swift kick in the pants.* (Brochure). (Available from American Mental Health Fund, P. O. Box 17389, Washington, DC 20041).

American Psychiatric Association. (1985, March). *Facts about teen suicide.* Washington, DC: Author.

American Psychiatric Association (1987). *Diagnostic and statistical manual of mental disorders* (3rd ed., rev.). Washington, DC: Author.

Anderson, D. R. (1981). Diagnosis and prediction of suicidal risk among adolescents. In C. F. Wells & I. R. Stuart (Eds.), *Self-destructive behavior in children and adolescents* (pp. 45–59). New York: Van Nostrand Reinhold.

Anderson, L. S. (1981). Notes on the linkage between the sexually abused child and the suicidal adolescent. *Journal of Adolescence, 4,* 157–162.

Anderson, R. (1986, September). Youth stress, suicide targets of board action. *Education Update, 21*(1), p. 1.

Anthony, E. J. (1975). Childhood depression. In E. J. Anthony & T. Benedek (Eds.), *Depression and human existence* (pp. 231–277). Boston: Little, Brown.

Anthony, E. J., & Cohler, B. J. (1987). *The invulnerable child.* New York: Guilford.

Asberg, M., Traskman, L., & Thoren, P. (1976). 5-HIAA in the cerebrospinal fluid: A biochemical suicide predictor? *Archives of General Psychiatry, 33*, 1193–1197.

Baechler, J. (1979). *Suicides*. New York: Basic Books.

Barraclough, B. (1973). Differences between national suicide rates. *British Journal of Psychiatry, 120*, 267–273.

Barter, J. T., Swaback, D. O., & Todd, D. (1968). Adolescent suicide attempts: A follow-up study of hospitalized patients. *Archives of General Psychiatry, 19*(5), 523–527.

Beck, A. T., Steer, R. A., Kovacs, M., & Garrison, B. (1985). Hopelessness and eventual suicide: A 10-year prospective study of patients hospitalized with suicidal ideation. *American Journal of Psychiatry, 142*, 559–563.

Bell, A., & Weinberg, M. (1978). *Homosexualities: A study of diversities among men and women*. New York: Simon & Schuster.

Bender, L., & Schilder, P. (1937). Suicidal preoccupations and attempts in children. *American Journal of Orthopsychiatry, 7*, 225–235.

Berkovitz, I. H. (1985). The role of schools in child, adolescent, and youth suicide prevention. In M. L. Peck, N. L. Farberow, & R. E. Litman (Eds.), *Youth suicide* (pp. 170–190). New York: Springer Publishing Company.

Berlin, I. N. (1979). Some implications of the developmental processes for treatment of depression in adolescence. In A. French & I. N. Berlin (Eds.), *Depression in children and adolescents* (pp. 87–108). New York: Human Sciences Press.

Berman, A. (1986). *Epidemiology of youth suicide*. Unpublished manuscript.

Bernstein, D. M. (1971). After transplantation—the child's emotional reactions. *American Journal of Psychiatry, 127*, 1189–1193.

Bible, C., & French, A. P. (1979). Depression in the child abuse syndrome. In A. P. French & I. N. Berlin (Eds.), *Depression in children and adolescents* (pp. 184–209). New York: Human Sciences Press.

Blaine, G. B., & Carmen, L. R (1968). Causal factors in suicidal attempts male and female college students. *American Journal of Psychiatry, 125*, 834–837.

Bloom, B. S. (1980, January). The new direction in educational research: Alterable variables. *Phi Delta Kappan, 61*(5), 382–385.

Blumenthal, S. (1985, April 30). *Testimony before the United States Senate Subcommittee on Juvenile Justice*. Washington, DC: U.S. Department of Health and Human Services.

Bollen, K. A., & Phillips, D. P. (1982, December). Imitative suicides. *American Sociological Review, 47*, 802–809.

Breed, W. (1970). The Negro and fatalistic suicide. *Pacific Sociological Review, 13*, 156–162.

Bronfenbrenner, U. (1986, February). Alienation and the four worlds of childhood. *Phi Delta Kappan, 67*(6), 430–436.

Brown, B. S., & Courtless, T. F. (1982). *The mentally retarded offender*. Washington, DC: National Institute of Mental Health.

Brown, G. L., Ebert, M. H., Goyer, P. F., Jimerson, D. C., Klein, W. J., Bunney, W. E., & Goodwin, F. K. (1982). Aggression, suicide, and serotonin: Relationship to CSF amine metabolites. *American Journal of Psychiatry, 139*, 741–746.

Brown, S. L. (1985). Adolescents and family systems. In M. L. Peck, N. L. Farberow, & R. E. Litman (Eds.), *Youth suicide* (pp. 48–70). New York: Springer Publishing Company.

Brumback, R. A., Staton, R. D., & Wilson, H. (1980). Neuropsychological study of children during and after remission of endogenous depressive episodes. *Perceptual and Motor Skills, 50,* 1163–1167.

Bryan, D. P., & Herjanic, B. (1980, August). Depression and suicide among adolescents and young adults with selective handicapping conditions. *Exceptional Education Quarterly, 1*(2), 57–65.

Cain, A. C. (Ed.). (1972). *Survivors of suicide.* Springfield, IL: Charles C Thomas.

Canfield, J., & Wells, H. C. (1976). *100 ways to enhance self-concept in the classroom.* Englewood Cliffs, NJ: Prentice-Hall.

Cantor, P. (1985, April 30). *Testimony on behalf of the Handgun Information Center before the Subcommittee on Juvenile Justice of the United States Senate Committee on the Judiciary.* Washington, DC: U.S. Department of Health and Human Services.

Cantwell, D. P. (1982). Childhood depression: A review of recent research. In B. B. Lahey & A. E. Kazdin (Eds.), *Advances in clinical child psychology* (Vol. 5, pp. 39–94). New York: Plenum.

Carlson, G. A., & Cantwell, D. P. (1982). Suicidal behavior and depression in children and adolescents. *Journal of the American Academy of Child Psychiatry, 21,* 361–368.

Centers for Disease Control. (1985). *Suicide surveillance, 1970–1980.* Atlanta, GA: U.S. Department of Health and Human Services.

Centers for Disease Control. (1986, November). *Youth suicide in the United States, 1970–1980.* Atlanta, GA: U.S. Department of Health and Human Services.

Charle, S. (1981, August). Suicide in the cellblocks: New programs attack the No. 1 killer of jail inmates. *Corrections Magazine, 7*(4), 6–16.

Child abuse and the handicapped child. (1987). (ERIC Digest #446). ERIC Clearinghouse on Handicapped and Gifted Children, 1920 Association Drive, Reston, VA 22091.

Clarizio, H. F., & McCoy, G. F. (1983). *Behavior disorders in children.* New York: Harper & Row.

Coffey, O. D. (1983). Meeting the needs of youth from a corrections viewpoint. In S. Braaten, R. B. Rutherford, Jr., & C. A. Kardash (Eds.), *Programming for adolescents with behavioral disorders* (Vol 1, pp. 79–84). Reston, VA: Council for Children with Behavioral Disorders.

Cohen-Sandler, R., Berman, A. L., & King, R. A. (1982). Life stress and symptomatology: Determinants of suicidal behavior in children. *Journal of the American Academy of Child Psychiatry, 21,* 178–186.

Coleman, L. (1986, March). Teen suicide clusters and the Werther effect. *The Network News: The Runaway Suicide Prevention Network Newsletter.*

Coleman, L. (1987). *Suicide clusters.* Boston: Faber & Faber.

Connell, P. H. (1965). Suicide in childhood. In G. Howells (Ed.), *Modern perspectives in child psychiatry* (pp. 403–425). Edinburgh: Oliver & Boyd.

Connell, H. M. (1972). Attempted suicide in school children. *Medical Journal of Australia, 1,* 686–690.

Conrad, D. (1986, April 13). Young children can also fall victim to severe depression. *St. Petersburg Times,* p. 4F.

Coopersmith, S. (1967). *The antecedents of self-esteem.* San Francisco: W. H. Freeman & Company.

Corder, B. F., & Haislip, T. M. (1983). Recognizing suicidal behavior in children. *Resident and Staff Physician, 29,* 18–23.

Cosand, B. J., Bourque, L. B., & Kraus, J. F. (1982). Suicide among adolescents in Sacramento County, California 1950–1959. *Adolescence, 17,* 917–930.

Crain, R. L., Mahard, R. E., & Narot, R. E. (1982). *Making desegregation work: How schools create social climates.* Cambridge, MA: Ballinger Publishing.

Cuniberti, B. (1983, July 10). Doctor calls for more suicide research. *Tampa Tribune-Times,* p. 12A.

Curphey, T. J. (1968, December). The psychological autopsy. *Bulletin of Suicidology,* 39–45.

Cytryn, L., & McKnew, D. H. (1972). Proposed classification of childhood depression. *American Journal of Psychiatry, 129*(2), 149.

Cytryn, L., & McKnew, D. H. (1974). Factors influencing the changing clinical expression of the depressive process in children. *American Journal of Psychiatry, 131*(8), 879.

Cytryn, L., & McKnew, D. H. (1980). Affective disorders of childhood. In H. K. Kaplan, A. M. Freedman, & R. Sadock (Eds.), *Comprehensive textbook of psychiatry* (3rd. ed., pp. 2798–2809). Baltimore: Williams & Wilkins.

Cytryn, L. McKnew, D. H., & Bunney, W. E. (1980). Diagnosis of depression in children: A reassessment. *American Journal of Psychiatry, 137*(1), 22–25.

Davidson, D. G., & Eastham, W. N. (1966). Acute liver necrosis following overdose of paracetamol. *British Medical Journal, 2,* 497–499.

Davis, J. M. (1985). Suicidal crises in schools. *School Psychology Review, 14*(3), 313–324.

deCatanzaro, D. (1981). *Suicide and self-damaging behavior: A sociological perspective.* New York: Academic Press.

Delisle, J. R. (1982). Striking out: Suicide and the gifted adolescent. *The Gifted Child Today (GCT), 24,* 16–19.

Delisle, J. R. (1986). Death with honors: Suicide among gifted adolescents. *Journal of Counseling and Development, 64*(a), 558–560.

Dorpat, T. L., Jackson, J., & Ripley, H. (1965). Broken homes and attempted and completed suicide. *Archives of General Psychiatry, 12*(2), 213–216.

Douglas, J. (1967). *The social meanings of suicide.* Princeton, NJ: Princeton University Press.

Drye, R. C. , Goulding, R. L., & Goulding, M. E. (1973). No suicide decisions, patient monitoring of suicidal risks. *American Journal of Psychiatry, 130*(2), 171–174.

Dublin, L. I. (1963). *Suicide: A sociological and statistical study.* New York: Ronald Press.

Dublin, L. I. (1969). Suicide prevention. In E. S. Shneidman (Ed.), *On the nature of suicide* (pp. 43–47). San Francisco: Jossey-Bass.

Dublin, L. I., & Bunzel, B. (1933). *To be or not to be: A study of suicide.* New York: Random House.

Durkheim, E. (1897). *Le suicide*. Paris: Libraire Felix Alcan. [G. Simpson (Ed.). Glencoe, IL: Free Press, 1951].

Dyer, J. A., & Kreitman, N. (1984). Hopelessness, depression, and suicidal intent. *British Journal of Psychiatry, 144,* 127–133.

Educating the gifted and talented. (1987, June). *FTP/NEA Advocate,* p. 5.

Eggleston, C. (1984). *Results of a national correctional/special education survey.* Paper presented at the Correctional/Special Education National Conference, Arlington, VA.

Eisenberg, L. (1980). Adolescent suicide: On taking arms against a sea of troubles. *Pediatrics, 66,* 315–320.

Eisenberg, L. (1984). The epidemiology of suicide in adolescents. *Pediatric Annals, 13,* 47–54.

Eisenberg, L. (1986). Does bad news about suicide beget bad news? *The New England Journal of Medicine, 315*(11), 705–707.

Elkind, D. (1981). *The hurried child.* Reading, MA: Addison-Wesley.

Erikson, E. H. (1964). *Childhood and society* (rev. ed.). New York: Norton.

Esquirol, J. E. (1838). *Des maladies mentales.* Paris: J. B. Bailliere.

Fagen, S., Long, N., & Stevens, D. (1975). *Teaching children self-control.* Columbus, OH: Charles E. Merrill.

Family services: A new frontier. (1986). *Special needs report, 1*(1), Akron, OH: Children's Hospital Medical Center of Akron. (Available from Family Child Learning Center, 281 Locust Street, Akron, Ohio 44308).

Farberow, N. L. (1969). *Bibliography on suicide and suicide prevention, 1897–1967.* Washington, DC: U.S. Government Printing Office.

Farberow, N. L. (1980). Indirect self-destructive behavior: Classification and characteristics. In N. L. Farberow (Ed.), *The many faces of suicide: Indirect self-destructive behavior* (pp. 16–27). New York: McGraw-Hill.

Farberow, N. L. (1985). Youth suicide: A summary. In M. L. Peck, N. L. Farberow, & R. E. Litman (Eds.), *Youth suicide* (pp. 191–203). New York: Springer.

Fawcett, J. A., & Susman, P. (1975). The clinical assessment of acute suicidal potential: A review. *Rush Presbyterian St. Luke's Medical Bulletin, 14,* 86–104.

Federal Register. (1977, August 23). Washington, DC: U.S. Government Printing Office.

Finch, S., & Poznanski, E. (1971). *Adolescent suicide.* Springfield, IL: Charles C Thomas.

Fowler, R. C., Rich, C. L., & Young, D. (1986). San Diego suicide study II: Substance abuse in young cases. *Archives of General Psychiatry, 43,* 962–965.

Frederick, C. J. (1978). Current trends in suicidal behavior in the United States. *American Journal of Psychotherapy, 32*(2), 172–200.

Frederick, C. J. (1985). An introduction and overview of youth suicide. In M. L. Peck, N. L. Farberow, & R. E. Litman (Eds.), *Youth suicide* (pp. 1–16). New York: Springer.

Frederick, C. J., & Resnick, H. L. (1971). How suicidal behaviors are learned. *American Journal of Psychotherapy, 25*(1), 37–55.

Freud, A., & Burlingham, D. (1944). *Infants without families.* New York: International Universities Press.

Friedman, P. (Ed.). (1967). *On suicide*. New York: International Universities Press.

Friedman, P. (1969). An individual act. In E. S. Shneidman (Ed.), *On the nature of suicide* (pp. 48–52). San Francisco: Jossey-Bass.

Gadow, K. D. (1986). *Children on medication* (Vol. II). Reston, VA: The Council for Exceptional Children.

Garfinkel, B. D., Froese, A., & Golumbek, H. (1979). Suicidal behaviour in a paediatric population. In *Proceedings of the 10th International Congress for Suicide Prevention and Crisis Intervention*, 305–312.

Garfinkel, B. D., Froese, A., & Hood, J. (1982). Suicide attempts in children and adolescents. *American Journal of Psychiatry, 139*, 1257–1261.

Garfinkel, B. D., & Golumbek, H. (1974). Suicide and depression in children and adolescents. *Canadian Medical Association Journal, 110*, 1278–1281.

Gastil, R. (1971). Homicide and a regional culture of violence. *American Sociological Review, 36*, 412–427.

Geller, B., Chestnut, E. C., Miller, M. D., Price, D. T., & Yates, E. (1985). Preliminary data on DSM-III associated features of major depressive disorder in children and adolescents. *American Journal of Psychiatry, 142*, 643–644.

Gerler, E. R. (1986, February). Skills for adolescence: A new program for young teenagers. *Phi Delta Kappan, 67*(6), 436–439.

Gerler, E. R., Jr., & Locke, D. C. (1980, November). Multimodal education: A model with promise. *Phi Delta Kappan, 61*, 214–215.

Getz, W. L., Allen, D. B., Myers, R. K., & Lindner, K. C. (1983). *Brief counseling with suicidal persons*. Lexington, MA: D.C. Heath.

Giffin, M., & Fesenthal, C. (1982). *A cry for help*. New York: Doubleday.

Giovacchini, P. (1981). *The urge to die: Why young people commit suicide*. New York: MacMillan.

Glasser, M., Amdur, M. J., & Backstrand, J. (1985, April). The impact of psychotherapists and primary physicians on suicide and other violent deaths in a rural area. *Canadian Journal of Psychiatry*, 195–201.

Glasser, W. (1986). *Control theory in the classroom*. New York: Harper & Row.

Goleman, D. (1987, October 20). Resilient kids: Why some thrive despite environment. *St. Petersburg Times*, pp. 1D, 4D.

Golumbek, H., & Garfinkel, B. D. (1983). *The adolescent and mood disturbance*. New York: International Universities Press.

Gould, M. S., & Shaffer, D. (1986). The impact of suicide in television movies: Evidence of imitation. *New England Journal of Medicine, 315*(11), 690–694.

Gould, M. S., Shaffer, D., & Kleinman, M. (1988, Spring). The impact of suicide in television movies: Replication and commentary. *Suicide and Life-Threatening Behavior, 18*(1), 90–99.

Gould, R. E. (1965). Suicide problems in children and adolescents. *American Journal of Psychotherapy, 19*, 228–246.

Green, A. H. (1968). Self-destructive behavior in physically abused schizophrenic children. *Archives of General Psychiatry, 19*, 171–179.

Green, A. H. (1978). Self-destructive behavior in battered children. *American Journal of Psychiatry, 135*, 579–582.

Greuling, J. W., & DeBlassie, R. R. (1980). Adolescent suicide. *Adolescence*, 15(59), 589–601.

Grief after suicide. (Available from Waukesha County Mental Health Association, Inc., 414 W. Moreland Blvd., Waukesha, WI 53186).

Grollman, E. A. (1971). *Suicide: Prevention, intervention, postvention*. Boston: Beacon Press.

Guetzloe, E. C. (1985a). The adolescent epidemic—suicide and depression: Education's responsibility. In J. E. Gilliam & B. K. Scott (Eds.), *Topics in emotional disturbance* (pp. 295–310). Austin, TX: Behavior Learning Center.

Guetzloe, E. C. (1985b, November). *The "Catch 22" of suicide prevention: Are we going too far?* Paper presented at the Ninth Annual Conference on Severe Behavior Disorders of Children and Youth, Scottsdale, AZ.

Guetzloe, E. C. (1987). *Suicide and depression, the adolescent epidemic: Education's responsibility* (rev. ed.). Orlando, FL: Advantage Consultants.

Guetzloe, E., & Johnson, D. (1985). *Suicide and depression, the adolescent epidemic: Education's responsibility* (abr. ed.). Orlando, FL: Advantage Consultants.

Guetzloe, E. C., & Rhodes, W. C. (1986, November). *Suicide prevention in the schools: Current trends and promising practices*. Paper presented at the 10th Annual Conference on Severe Behavior Disorders of Children and Youth.

Guetzloe, E. C., & Rhodes, W. C. (1988). Prevention of youth suicide: Current trends and promising practices. In R. Rutherford, C. M. Nelson, & S. R. Forness (Eds.), *Bases of severe behavior disorders in children and youth* (pp. 231–250). San Diego: College-Hill Press.

Guinn, L. (1989, May). *Strategies to reverse alienation*. Paper presented at the 1989 Conference on Contemporary Youth Issues, Austin, TX. (Available from Classroom Management and Discipline Program and Schools Against Substance Abuse, Southwest Texas State University, San Marcos, TX.)

Handgun Information Center (1984). *Let's keep handguns out of the wrong hands*. (Brochure). (Available from The Handgun Information Center, 1400 K Street, Suite 500, Washington, DC 20005).

Hart, N. A., & Keidel, G. C. (1979). The suicidal adolescent. *American Journal of Nursing, 79*, 80–84.

Havighurst, R. J. (1952). *Developmental tasks and education*. New York: Longmans.

Havighurst, R. J. (1969). Suicide and education. In E. S. Shneidman (Ed.), *On the nature of suicide* (pp. 53–67). San Francisco: Jossey-Bass.

Hawton, K. (1978). Deliberate self-poisoning and self-injury in the psychiatric hospital. *British Journal of Medical Psychology, 51*, 253–259.

Hawton, K. (1986). *Suicide and attempted suicide among children and adolescents*. Beverly Hills, CA: Sage Publications.

Hawton, K., & Catalan, J. (1982). *Attempted suicide: A practical guide to its nature and management*. Oxford: Oxford University Press.

Hawton, K., Cole, D., O'Grady, J., & Osborn, M. (1982). Motivational aspects of deliberate self–poisoning in adolescents. *British Journal of Psychiatry, 141*, 286–291.

Hawton, K., & Goldacre, M.(1982). Hospital admissions for adverse effects of medicinal agents (mainly self-poisoning) among adolescents in the Oxford region. *British Journal of Psychiatry, 141*, 106–170.

Hawton, K., O'Grady, J., Osborn, M., & Cole, D. (1982). Adolescents who take overdoses: Their characteristics, problems, and contacts with helping agencies. *British Journal of Psychiatry, 140,* 118–123.

Headlam, H. K., Goldsmith, J., Hanenson, I. B., & Rauh, J. L. (1979). Demographic characteristics of adolescents with self-poisoning. *Clinical Pediatrics, 18,* 147–154.

Hellon, C. P., & Solomon, M. I. (1980). Suicide and age in Alberta, Canada, 1951–1977: The changing profile. *Archives of General Psychiatry, 37,* 505–510.

Hendin, H. (1975a). Growing up dead: Student suicide. *American Journal of Psychotherapy, 29*(3), 327–338.

Hendin, H. (1975b). Student suicide: Death as a lifestyle. *Journal of Nervous and Mental Diseases, 160*(3), 204–219.

Hendin, H. (1980). *Suicide in the adolescent and youth.* Paper presented at the Suicide Prevention Center Symposium on Youth Suicide, Los Angeles, CA.

Hendin, H. (1982). *Suicide in America.* New York: W. W. Norton.

Hendin, H. (1985). Suicide among the young: Psychodynamics and demography. In M. L. Peck, N. L. Farberow, & R. E. Litman (Eds.), *Youth suicide* (pp. 19–38). New York: Springer.

Henry, A. F., & Short, J. F., Jr. (1954). *Suicide and homicide.* New York: MacMillan.

Heredity, chemical imbalance tied to teen suicide. (1987, May 14). *St. Petersburg Times,* p. 3A.

Hidlay, W. C. (1988, September 14). 30% of teens have thought about suicide. *St. Petersburg Times,* p. 18A.

Hildebrand, J. (1987, March 16). School is sued over teen-ager's suicide. *The Richmond News Leader,* p. 2.

Jacobs, J. (1971). *Adolescent suicide.* Toronto: Wiley & Sons.

Jacobs, J., & Teicher, J. (1967). Broken homes and social isolation in attempted suicides of adolescents. *International Journal of Social Psychiatry, 13*(2), 139–149.

Jacobson, S., & Faegre, C. (1969). Neutralization: A tool for the classroom teacher. In H. Dupont (Ed.), *Educating emotionally disturbed children* (pp. 249–254). New York: Holt, Rinehart, & Winston.

Jacobziner, H. (1965). Attempted suicide in adolescents. *Journal of the American Medical Association, 161,* 101–105.

Jan-Tausch, J. (1964). *Suicide of children 1960–1963.* New Jersey Public Schools, Division of Curriculum and Instruction—Office of Special Education Services, Department of Education, Trenton, New Jersey.

Jobes, D. A., Berman, A. L., & Josselsen, A. R. (1986, January). The impact of psychological autopsies on medical examiners determination of manner of death. *Journal of Forensic Science, 31*(1), 177–189.

Jones, V. F. (1980). *Adolescents with behavior problems: Strategies for teaching, counseling, and parent involvement.* Boston: Allyn & Bacon.

Jourard, S. M. (1969). The invitation to die. In E. S. Shneidman (Ed.), *On the nature of suicide* (pp. 129–141). San Francisco: Jossey-Bass.

Joyce, B., & Showers, B. (1987, January). The power of schooling. *Phi Delta Kappan, 68*(5), 352–355.

Kahn, A. U., Herndon, C. H., & Ahmadian, S. Y. (1971). Social and emotional adaptations of children with transplanted kidneys and chronic hemodialysis. *American Journal of Psychiatry, 127,* 1194–1198.

Kashani, J. H., McGee, R. O., Clarkson, S. E., Anderson, J. C., Walton, L. A., Williams, S., Silva, P. A., Robins, A. J., Cytryn, L., & McKnew, D. H. (1983). Depression in a sample of 9 year old children. *Archives of General Psychiatry, 40,* 1217–1223.

Kashani, J. H., Venske, R., & Millar, E. A. (1981). Depression in children admitted to hospital for orthopedic procedures. *British Journal of Psychiatry, 138,* 21–25.

Kauffman, J. M. (1985). *Characteristics of children's behavior disorders* (3rd. ed.). Columbus, OH: Charles E. Merrill.

Kazdin, A. E., French, A. S., Unis, A. S., Esveldt-Dawson, K., & Sherick, R. B. (1983). Hopelessness, depression, and suicidal intent among psychiatrically disturbed inpatient children. *Journal of Consulting and Clinical Psychology, 51,* 504–510.

Kenny, T. J., Rohn, R., Sarles, R. M., Reynolds, B. J., & Heald, F. P. (1979). Visual-motor problems of adolescents who attempt suicide. *Perceptual and Motor Skills, 48,* 599–602.

Khantzian, E. J., & Mack, J. E. (1983). Self-preservation and the care of the self: Ego instincts reconsidered. *Psychoanalytic Study of the Child, 38,* 209–232.

Knoblock, P. (1983). *Teaching emotionally disturbed children.* Boston: Houghton Mifflin.

Koocher, G. P. (1973). Childhood, death, and cognitive development. *Developmental Psychology, 9*(3), 369–375.

Kosky, R. (1983). Childhood suicidal behavior. *Journal of Child Psychology and Psychiatry, 24*(3), 457–468.

Kreitman, N., Smith, P., & Tan, E. S. (1970). Attempted suicide as language: An empirical study. *British Journal of Psychiatry, 116,* 465–473.

Kubie, L. (1969). A complex process. In E. S. Shneidman (Ed.), *On the nature of suicide* (pp. 81–86). San Francisco: Jossey-Bass.

Lajoie, S., & Shore, B. M. (1981). Three myths? The over-representation of the gifted among dropouts, delinquents, and suicides. *Gifted Child Quarterly, 25,* 38–43.

Lazarus, A. A. (1978, October). What is multimodal therapy? A brief overview. *Elementary School Guidance and Counseling, 13*(1), 6–11.

Leroux, J. A. (1986). Suicidal behavior and gifted adolescents. *Roeper Review, 9*(2), 77–79.

Lesse, S. (Ed.). (1974). *Masked depression.* New York: Jason Aronson.

Levenson, M., & Neuringer, C. (1971). Problem-solving behavior in suicidal adolescents. *Journal of Consulting and Clinical Psychology, 37,* 433–436.

Lewis, A. (1956). Statistical aspects of suicide. *The Canadian Medical Association Journal, 74,* 99–104.

Litman, R. E. (1968, January). Psychological-psychiatric aspects in certifying modes of death. *Journal of Forensic Sciences, 13,* 46–54.

Litman, R. E. (1970). Suicide as acting out. In E. S. Shneidman, N. L. Farberow, & R. E. Litman (Eds.), *The psychology of suicide* (pp. 293–304). New York: Science House.

Litman, R. E. (1980). Psychodynamics of indirect self-destructive behavior. In N. F. Farberow (Ed.), *The many faces of suicide* (pp. 28–40). New York: McGraw-Hill.

Litman, R. E., & Diller, J. (1985). Case studies in youth suicide. In M. L. Peck, N. L. Farberow, & R. E. Litman (Eds.), *Youth suicide* (pp. 48–70). New York: Springer.

Lucianowicz, N. (1968). Attempted suicide in children. *Acta Psychiatrica Scandinavia, 44,* 415–435.

Lukens, E., Puig-Antich, J., Behn, J., Goetz, R., Tabrizi, M. A., & Davies, M. (1983). Reliability of the psychosocial schedule for school-age children. *Journal of the American Academy of Child Psychiatry, 22,* 29–39.

Luty, C. (1985, January/February). Suicidal students. *NEA Today,* pp. 4–5.

MacGregor, M. (1977). Juvenile diabetics growing up. *Lancet, 1,* 944–945.

Mack, J. E., & Hickler, H. (1981). *Vivienne.* Boston: Little, Brown.

Margolin, N., & Teicher, J. D. (1968). Thirteen adolescent male suicide attempters. *Journal of the American Academy of Child Psychiatry, 7,* 296–315.

Maris, R. (1969). *Social forces in urban suicide.* Homewood, IL: Dorsey Press.

Maris, R. (1981). *Pathways to suicide.* Baltimore: The Johns Hopkins University Press.

Marks, A., & Abernathy, T. (1974). Toward a sociocultural perspective on means of self-destruction. *Suicide and Life-threatening Behavior, 4,* 3–17.

Marks, P. A., & Haller, D. L. (1977). Now I lay me down for keeps: A study of adolescent suicide attempts. *Journal of Clinical Psychology, 33,* 390–400.

Maslow, A. (1954). *Motivation and personality.* New York: Harper & Row.

Maslow, A. (1962). *Toward a psychology of being.* Princeton, NJ: D. Van Nostrand Company, Inc.

Mason, D. (1985, December 16). Adolescent suicide. *St. Petersburg Times,* pp. 1D–2D.

Matter, D., & Matter, R. (1984). Suicide among elementary school children: A serious concern for counselors. *Elementary School Guidance and Counseling, 18,* 260–267.

Mattson, A., Seese, L. R., & Hawkins, J. W. (1969). Suicidal behavior as a child psychiatric emergency: Clinical characteristics and follow-up results. *Archives of General Psychiatry, 20,* 100–109.

McCants, G. F. (1985). Suicide among the gifted. *The Gifted Child Today (GCT), 38,* 27–29.

McClure, G. M. (1984). Recent trends in suicide amongst the young. *British Journal of Psychiatry, 144,* 134–138.

McCormack, P. (1985, February 10). Who'll survive suicide show? *The Edmonton Sunday Sun,* p. A1.

McIntyre, M. S., & Angle, C. R. (1973). Psychological "biopsy" in self-poisoning of children and adolescents. *American Journal of Diseases of Children, 126,* 42–46.

McIntyre, M. S., & Angle, C. R. (1981). The taxonomy of suicide and self-poisoning—A pediatric perspective. In C. F. Wells & I. R. Stuart (Eds.), *Self-destructive behavior in children and adolescents* (pp. 224–249). New York: Van Nostrand Reinhold.

McIntyre, M. S., Angle, C. R., & Schlicht, M. L. (1977). Suicide and self-poisoning in pediatrics. *Advances in Pediatrics, 24,* 291–310.

McKenry, P. C., Tishler, C. L., & Christman, K. L. (1980, March). Adolescent suicide and the classroom teacher. *The Journal of School Health, 50,* 130–132.

Menninger, K. (1933). Psychoanalytic aspects of suicide. *International Journal of Psycho-Analysis, 14,* 376–390.

Miller, J. P. (1975). Suicide in adolescence. *Adolescence, 10*(37), 11–24.

Miller, H. L., Coombs, D. W., Leeper, J. D., & Barton, S. N. (1984). An analysis of the effects of suicide prevention facilities on suicide rates in the United States. *American Journal of Public Health, 74,* 340–343.

Minneapolis Public Schools. (1986, February 12). *Student suicide prevention guidelines.* (Available from Minneapolis Public Schools, School Social Work Services, Minneapolis, MN.)

Mishara, B. L. (1979). Suicidal verbalizations and attempts in college students: A multivariate log-linear analysis of the perceived helplessness of peer reactions. In *Proceedings of the 10th International Congress for Suicide Prevention* (p. 328). Ottawa, Canada: International Association for Suicide Prevention, Inc.

Morgan, D. J. (1979). Prevalence and types of handicapping conditions found in juvenile correctional institutions: A national survey. *Journal of Special Education, 13,* 283–295.

Morrison, G., & Collier, J. (1969). Family treatment approaches to suicidal children and adolescents. *Journal of the American Academy of Child Psychiatry, 8*(1), 140–153.

Morse, W. C., Ardizzone, J., MacDonald, C., & Pasick, P. (1980). *Affective education for special children and youth.* Reston, VA: The Council for Exceptional Children.

Motto, J. A. (1985). Treatment concerns in preventing youth suicide. In M. L. Peck, N. L. Farberow, & R. E. Litman (Eds.), *Youth suicide* (pp. 91–111). New York: Springer.

Murphy, G. E., & Wetzel, R. D. (1982). Family history of suicidal behavior among suicide attempters. *Journal of Nervous and Mental Disease, 170,* 86–90.

Myers, K. M., Burke, P., & McCauley, E. (1985). Suicidal behavior by hospitalized preadolescent children on a psychiatric unit. *Journal of the American Academy of Child Psychiatry, 24,* 474–480.

Nagy, M. (1948). The child's theories concerning death. *Journal of Genetic Psychology, 73,* 3–27.

National Center for Health Statistics (1987, August 28). *Advance report of final mortality statistics, 1985.* [Monthly Vital Statistics Report, Vol. 36, No. 5, Supplementary DHHS Publication No. (PHS) 87–1120]. Hyattsville, MD: U.S. Public Health Service.

National Institute on Drug Abuse. (1985). *Indicators of suicide and depression among drug abusers.* (DHHS Publication No. ADM 85–1411) Washington, DC: U.S. Government Printing Office.

Nilson, P. (1981). Psychological profiles of runaway children and adolescents. In C. F. Wells & I. R. Stuart (Eds.), *Self-destructive behavior in children and adolescents* (pp. 2–43). New York: Van Nostrand Reinhold.

Ninan, P. T., Van Kammen, D. P., Scheinen, M., Linnoila, M., Bunney, W. E., & Goodwin, F. K. (1984). CSF 5-hydroxyindoleacetic acid levels in suicidal schizophrenic patients. *American Journal of Psychiatry, 141,* 566–569.

Orbach, I., & Glaubman, H. (1978). Suicidal, aggressive and normal children's perception of personal and impersonal death. *Journal of Clinical Psychology, 34,* 850–857.

Otto, U. (1972). Suicidal acts by children and adolescents. *Acta Psychiatrica Scandinavia,* Supplement 233.

Pardes, H. (1985). Foreword. In M. L. Peck, N. L. Farberow, & R. E. Litman (Eds.), *Youth suicide* (pp. vii–xi). New York: Springer.

Parental involvement called essential to good education. (1987, June). *FTP/NEA Advocate,* p. 12.

Paykel, E. S., Myers, J. H., Lindenthal, J. J., & Tanner, J. (1974). Suicidal feelings in the general population: A prevalence study. *British Journal of Psychiatry, 124,* 460–469.

Peck, M. (1982). Youth suicide. *Death Education, 6,* 29–47.

Peck, M. L. (1968). Suicide motivation in adolescents. *Adolescence, 3*(9), 109–117.

Peck, M. L. (1981). In S. C. Feinstein, J. G. Looney, A. Z. Schwartzberg, & A. D. Sorosky (Eds.), *Adolescent psychiatry* (Vol. 9, pp. 461–467). Chicago: University of Chicago Press.

Peck, M. L. (1985). Crisis intervention treatment with chronically and acutely suicidal adolescents. In M. L. Peck, N. L. Farberow, & R. E. Litman (Eds.), *Youth suicide* (pp. 112–122). New York: Springer.

Peck, M. L., & Schrut, A. S. (1971, February). Suicidal behavior among college students. *HSMHA Health Reports, 86*(2), 149–156.

Perlin, S. (Ed.). (1975). *A handbook for the study of suicide.* New York: Oxford University Press.

Pfeffer, C. R. (1978). Hospital treatment of suicidal latency age children. *Suicide and Life-threatening Behavior, 8,* 150–160.

Pfeffer, C. R. (1980). Parental suicide: An organizing event in the development of latency-age children. *Suicide and Life-threatening Behavior, 11,* 43–50.

Pfeffer, C. R. (1981). The distinctive features of children who threaten and commit suicide. In C. F. Wells & I. R. Stuart (Eds.), *Self-destructive behavior in children and adolescents* (pp. 106–120). New York: Van Nostrand Reinhold.

Pfeffer, C. R. (1983). *Preoccupations with death in "normal" children: The relationship to suicidal behavior.* Paper presented at a symposium of The Foundation of Thanatology, New York.

Pfeffer, C. R. (1984). Clinical aspects of suicidal behavior. *Pediatric Annals, 13,* 56–61.

Pfeffer, C. R. (1985). Suicidal fantasies in normal children. *The Journal of Nervous and Mental Disease, 173*(2), 78–84.

Pfeffer, C. R. (1986). *The suicidal child.* New York: The Guilford Press.

Pfeffer, C. R., Conte, H. R., Plutchik, R., & Jerrett, I. (1979). Suicidal behavior in latency-age children: An empirical study. *Journal of the American Academy of Child Psychiatry, 18,* 679–692.

Pfeffer, C. R., Conte, H. R., Plutchik, R., & Jerrett, I. (1980). Suicidal behavior in latency-age children: An empirical study: An outpatient population. *Journal of the American Academy of Child Psychiatry, 19,* 703–710.

Pfeffer, C. R., & Plutchik, R. (1982). Psychopathology of latency-age children: Relation to treatment planning. *Journal of Nervous and Mental Disease, 17,* 193–197.

Pfeffer, C. R., Plutchik, R., Mizruchi, M.S., & Lipkins, R. (1985). *Suicidal behavior in child psychiatric inpatients, outpatients, and nonpatients.* Paper presented at the Annual Meeting of the American Psychiatric Association, Dallas.

Pfeffer, C. R., Solomon, G., Plutchik, R., Mizruchi, M. S., & Weiner, A. (1982). Suicidal behavior in latency-age psychiatric patients: A replication and cross-validation. *Journal of the American Academy of Child Psychiatry, 21,* 564–569.

Pfeffer, C. R., Zuckerman, S., Plutchik, R., & Mizruchi, M. S. (1984). Suicidal behavior in normal school children: A comparison with child psychiatric patients. *Journal of the American Academy of Child Psychiatry, 23*(4), 416–423.

Phillips, D. P. (1974). The influence of suggestion on suicide: Substantive and theoretical implications of the Werther effect. *American Sociological Review, 39,* 340–354.

Phillips, D. P. (1979). Suicide, motor fatalities, and the mass media: Evidence toward a theory of suggestion. *American Journal of Sociology, 84,* 1150–1174.

Phillips, D. P., & Carstensen, L. L. (1986, September 11). Clustering of teenage suicides after television news stories about suicide. *New England Journal of Medicine, 315*(11), 685–689.

Phillips, D. P., & Paight, D. J. (1987). The impact of televised movies about suicide: A replicative study. *New England Journal of Medicine, 317,* 809–811.

Podhoretz, N. (1987, March 28). Teach kids life is worth the pain. *Minneapolis Star & Tribune,* p. 18A.

Public Health Service, U.S. Department of Health and Human Services. (1980). *Promoting health/preventing disease: Objectives for the nation.* Washington, DC: U.S. Government Printing Office.

Puig-Antich, J. (1980). Affective disorders in childhood: A review and perspective. *Psychiatric Clinics of North America, 3,* 403–424.

Puig-Antich, J. (1982). Major depressive and conduct disorder in prepuberty. *Journal of the American Academy of Child Psychiatry, 21,* 118–128.

Puig-Antich, J. (1986). Psychobiological markers: Effects of age and puberty. In M. Rutter, C. E. Izard, & P. B. Read (Eds.), *Depression in young people* (pp. 341–381). New York: Guilford Press.

Reasoner, R. W. (1982). *Building self-esteem.* Palo Alto, CA: Consulting Psychologists Press.

Researcher says teen suicide rate going down. (1986, October 1). *St. Petersburg Times,* p. 13A.

Rhodes, W. C., & Guetzloe, E. C. (1987, November). *Consciousness construction and the changing curriculum paradigm.* Paper presented at the 11th Annual Conference on Severe Behavior Disorders of Children and Youth, Tempe, AZ.

Richman, J. (1981). Family treatment of suicidal children and adolescents. In

C. F. Wells & I. R. Stuart (Eds.), *Self-destructive behavior in children and adolescents* (pp. 274–290). New York: Van Nostrand Reinhold.

Richman, J. (1986). *Family therapy for suicidal people.* New York: Springer.

Ring, J. (1984, September). Teenage suicide. *Westchester Spotlight,* pp. 1–3.

Ritter, M. (1988, May 12). Teenagers and suicide. *St. Petersburg Times,* p. 15A.

Robbins, D. R., & Alessi, N. E. (1985). Depressive symptoms and suicidal behavior in adolescents. *American Journal of Psychiatry, 142*(5), 588–592.

Roesler, T., & Deisher, R. W. (1972). Youthful male homosexuality: Homosexual experience and the process of developing homosexual identity in males 16 to 22 years. *Journal of the American Medical Association, 219*(8), 1018–1023.

Rohn, R. D., Sarles, R. M., Kenny, T. J., Reynolds, B. J., & Heald, F. P. (1977). Adolescents who attempt suicide. *Journal of Pediatrics, 90*(4), 636–638.

Rosen, G. (1975). History. In S. Perlin (Ed.), *A handbook for the study of suicide* (pp. 3–29). New York: Oxford University Press.

Rosenkrantz, A. L. (1978). A note on adolescent suicide: Incidence, dynamics, and some suggestions for treatment. *Adolescence, 13,* 209–214.

Rosenthal, P. A., & Rosenthal, S. (1984). Suicidal behavior by preschool children. *American Journal of Psychiatry, 141,* 520–525.

Ross, C. (1985). Teaching children the facts of life and death: Suicide prevention in the schools. In M. L. Peck, N. L. Farberow, & R. E. Litman (Eds.), *Youth suicide* (pp. 147–169). New York: Springer.

Ross, C. P. (1980). Mobilizing schools for suicide prevention. *Suicide and Life-threatening Behavior, 10*(4), 239–243.

Rumack, B. H. (1983). Acetaminophen overdose. *American Journal of Medicine, 75,* 104–112.

Rutherford, R. B., Jr., Nelson, C. M., & Wofford, B. I. (1985). Special education in the most restrictive environment: Correctional special education. *Journal of Special Education, 19,* 59–71.

Rutter, M. (1986). The developmental psychopathology of depression. In M. Rutter, C. E. Izard, & P. B. Read (Eds.). *Depression in young people* (pp. 3–30). New York: Guilford.

Sabbath, J. C. (1969). The suicidal adolescent—the expendable child. *Journal of the American Academy of Child Psychiatry, 8,* 272–289.

Sagher, M. T., & Robins, E. (1971). Male and female homosexuality: Natural history. *Comprehensive Psychiatry, 12*(6), 503–510.

Salk, L., Lipsitt, L. P., Sturner, W. Q., Reilly, B. M., & Levat, R. H. (1985, March 16). Relationship of maternal and perinatal conditions to eventual adolescent suicide. *The Lancet, 1,* 624–627.

Santamour, M. B., & West, B. (1979). Retardation and criminal justice: A training manual for criminal justice personnel. Washington, DC: President's Committee on Mental Retardation.

Sathyavathi, K. (1975). Suicide among children in Bangalore. *Indian Journal of Paediatrics, 42,* 149–157.

Scanlan, C. (1987, December 1). Evidence of a new kind. *St. Petersburg Times,* pp. 1D–2D.

Schilder, P., & Wechsler, D. (1934). The attitudes of children toward death. *Journal of Genetic Psychology, 45,* 406–451.

Schlafly, P. (Ed.). (1985, February). *Child abuse in the classroom. Excerpts from official transcript of proceedings before the U.S. Department of Education* (2nd ed.). Alton, IL: Pere Marquette Press.

Schneer, N. L., Kay, P., & Brosovsky, M. (1961). Events and conscious ideation leading to suicidal behavior in adolescence. *Psychiatric Quarterly, 35,* 507–515.

School districts can be sued for inadequate suicide prevention programs. (1986, June). *The School's Advocate,* pp. 1–3.

Schools that rescue children. (1987, November 2). *St. Petersburg Times,* 12A.

Schrut, A. (1964). Suicidal adolescents and children. *Journal of the American Medical Association, 188,* 1103–1107.

Seiden, R. H. (1966). Campus tragedy: A study of student suicide. *Journal of Abnormal Psychology, 71*(6), 389–399.

Seiden, R. H. (1969). *Suicide among youth: A review of the literature, 1900–1967.* (PHS Pub. No. 1971). NIMH Bulletin of Suicidology (Supplement).

Shaffer, D. (1974). Suicide in childhood and early adolescence. *Journal of Child Psychology and Psychiatry, 15,* 275–291.

Shaffer, D. (1985). *Suicide and depression in children and adolescents.* Mimeo. New York: New York State Psychiatric Institute, Columbia College of Physicians and Surgeons.

Shaffer, D. (1986). Developmental factors in child and adolescent suicide. In M. Rutter, C. E. Izard, & P. B. Read (Eds.), *Depression in young people: Developmental and clinical perspectives* (pp. 383–396). New York: The Guilford Press.

Shaffer, D., & Fisher, P. (1981). Suicide in children and young adolescents. In C. F. Wells & I. R. Stuart (Eds.), *Self-destructive behavior in children and adolescents* (pp. 75–104). New York: Van Nostrand Reinhold.

Shaffi, M., Carrigan, S., Whittinghill, J. R., & Derrick, A. (1985). Psychological autopsy of completed suicide in children and young adolescents. *Journal of the American Academy of Child Psychiatry, 20,* 545–565.

Shedlin, A. Jr. (1986, October). New lenses for viewing elementary schools. *Phi Delta Kappan, 68*(2), 139–142.

Sheras, P. L. (1983). Suicide in adolescence. In C. E. Walker & M. C. Roberts (Eds.), *Handbook of clinical child psychology* (pp. 759–784). New York: Wiley.

Shneidman, E. S. (1966). Orientations toward death. *International Journal of Psychiatry, 2,* 167–174.

Shneidman, E. S. (1969). Fifty-eight years. In E. S. Shneidman (Ed.), *On the nature of suicide* (pp. 1–30). San Francisco: Jossey-Bass.

Shneidman, E. S. (1970a). Pioneer in suicidology. In E. S. Shneidman, N. L. Farberow, & R. E. Litman (Eds.), *The psychology of suicide* (pp. 627–629). New York: Science House.

Shneidman, E. S. (1970b). Preventing suicide. In E. S. Shneidman, N. L. Farberow, & R. E. Litman (Eds.), *The psychology of suicide* (pp. 429–440). New York: Science House.

Shneidman, E. S. (1970c). Recent developments in suicide prevention. In E. S. Shneidman, N. L. Farberow, & R. E. Litman (Eds.), *The psychology of suicide* (pp. 145–155). New York: Science House.

Shneidman, E. S. (1973a). *Deaths of man*. New York: New York Times Book Company.

Shneidman, E. S. (1973b). Suicide. In *Encyclopaedia Britannica*, Vol. 210 (pp. 383–386). Chicago: Benton.

Shneidman, E. S. (1975). Suicide. In A. M. Freedman, H. I. Kaplan, & B. J. Sadock (Eds.), *Comprehensive textbook of psychiatry–II* (Vol. 2, pp. 1774–1785). Baltimore: Williams & Wilkins.

Shneidman, E. S. (1985). *Definition of suicide*. New York: Wiley.

Shneidman, E. S., & Farberow, N.L. (1957). Some comparisons between genuine and simulated suicide notes. *Journal of General Psychology, 56,* 251–256.

Shneidman, E. S., & Farberow, N.L. (1961). Statistical comparisons between attempted and committed suicides. In N. L. Farberow & E. S. Shneidman (Eds.), *The cry for help* (pp. 19–47). New York: McGraw-Hill.

Shneidman, E. S., & Farberow, N. L. (1970). Sample psychological autopsies. In E. S. Shneidman, N. L. Farberow, & R. E. Litman (Eds.), *The psychology of suicide* (pp. 497–510). New York: Science House.

Shneidman, E. S., & Mandelkorn, P. (1970). How to prevent suicide. In E. S. Shneidman, N. L. Farberow, & R. E. Litman (Eds.), *The psychology of suicide* (pp. 125–143). New York: Science House.

Shoaff, S. (1985, July 21). Dungeons and dragons: Is death part of the game? *Clearwater Sun*, pp. 1A–2A.

Shrier, D., & Johnson, R. L. (1985). Problem behaviors of adolescence: A clinical perspective. *American Journal of Family Therapy, 13*(1), 72–75.

Silver, L. B. (1985, April 30). *Testimony before the United States Senate Subcommittee on Juvenile Justice*. Washington, DC: Public Health Service, U. S. Department of Health and Human Services.

Simpson, G. (1951). Editor's preface. In E. Durkheim, *Suicide: A study in sociology* (J. A. Spaulding & G. Simpson, Trans.) (pp. 9–12). New York: The Free Press.

Sobey, F. (1970). *The nonprofessional revolution in mental health*. New York: Columbia University Press.

Stanley, E. J., & Barter, J. T. (1970). Adolescent suicidal behavior. *American Journal of Orthopsychiatry, 40*(1), 87–93.

State of Florida. (1987). *Youth suicide prevention: A guide for trainers*. (Available from Prevention Center, Department of Education, Knott Building, 106 Winchester A, Tallahassee, FL 32399.)

Stengel, E. (1969). *Suicide and attempted suicide*. Baltimore: Penguin Books.

Stickney, S. B. (1968). Schools are our mental health centers. *Journal of the American Psychiatric Association, 124,* 101–108.

Strother, D. B. (1986, June). Practical applications of research: Suicide among the young. *Phi Delta Kappan, 67,* 756–759.

Suicide—part I. (1986, February). *Harvard Medical School Mental Health Letter, 2*(8), 1–4.

Suicide prevention in the schools. (1984, September). *Newslink, 10*(3), 1–2.

Survey finds one-third of teens consider suicide. (1989, March 10). *St. Petersburg Times*, 3A.

Taylor, E. A., & Stansfield, S. A. (1984). Children who poison themselves: Clinical comparison with psychiatric controls and prediction of attendance for treatment. *British Journal of Psychiatry, 145*, 127–135.

Taylor, R. L. (1984). *Assessment of exceptional students: Educational and psychological procedures.* Englewood Cliffs, NJ: Prentice-Hall.

Taylor, R. L. (1985, October). Measuring adaptive behavior: Issues and instruments. *Focus on Exceptional Children, 18*(2).

Taylor, S. (1982). *Durkheim and the study of suicide.* New York: St. Martin's Press.

Teen stress and suicide prevention project. (1988, Winter). Positive Directions. *Newsletter of the Ohio Council for Children with Behavioral Disorders.* (Available from OCCBD, 301 Obetz Road, Columbus, OH 43207).

Teicher, J. D., & Jacobs, J. (1966). Adolescents who commit suicide: Preliminary findings. *American Journal of Psychiatry, 122*(11), 1248–1257.

Tishler, C. L., & McKenry, P. C. (1982). Parental negative self and adolescent suicide attempts. *Journal of the American Academy of Child Psychiatry, 21*, 404–408.

Tishler, C. L., McKenry, P. C., & Morgan, K. C. (1981). Adolescent suicide attempts: Some significant factors. *Suicide and Life-threatening Behavior, 11*(2), 86–92.

Toolan, J. M. (1962). Depression in children and adolescents. *American Journal of Orthopsychiatry, 32*, 404–415.

Toolan, J. M. (1978). Therapy of depressed and suicidal children. *American Journal of Psychotherapy, 32*(2), 243–251.

Tsuang, M. T. (1977). Genetic factors in suicide. *Diseases of the Nervous System, 38*, 498–501.

Tuckman, J., & Connon, H. E. (1962). Attempted suicide in adolescents. *American Journal of Psychiatry, 119*, 228–232.

Tugend, A. (1984a, October 31). Researchers begin to examine suicide as national problem. *Education Week, 4*(9), pp. 12–13.

Tugend, A. (1984b, October 31). Suicide: Unsettling worry for schools. *Education Week, 4*(9), pp. 1, 12–13.

U.S. Public Health Service. (1980). *Promoting health/preventing disease: Objectives for the nation.* Washington, DC: U. S. Government Printing Office.

Varah, C. (1966). *The Samaritans.* New York: MacMillan.

Viadero, D. (1987, January 28). Panel to develop model suicide prevention program for schools. *Education Week, 4*(18), p. 5.

Viadero, D. (1987, October 28). Studies shed new light on teen-age suicides. *Education Week*, p. 7.

Vincent, L., Davis, J., Brown, P., Miller, J., & Gruenewald, L. (1983). *Parent inventory of child development in non-school environments.* (Available from Madison Metropolitan School District, Early Childhood Program, Madison, WI 53703).

Walberg, H. J. (1984, February). Families as partners in educational productivity. *Phi Delta Kappan, 65*(6), 397–400.

Wasserman, I. M. (1984). Imitation and suicide: A reexamination of the Werther effect. *American Sociological Review, 49*, 427–436.

Weiss, G., Minde, K., Werry, J. S., Douglas, V., & Nemeth, E. (1971). Studies on the hyperactive child: VIII. Five-year follow-up. *Archives of General Psychiatry, 24,* 409–418.

Weissberg, M. (1983). *Dangerous secrets: Maladaptive responses to stress.* New York: W. W. Norton.

Wellisch, D. K., & Ungerleider, J. T. (1985). Destructive aspects of the cult experience. In M. L. Peck, N. L. Farberow, & R. E. Litman (Eds.), *Youth suicide* (pp. 80–87). New York: Springer.

Wenz, F. V. (1979). Sociological correlates of alienation among adolescent suicide attempts. *Adolescence, 14,* 19–30.

Werner, E., & Smith, R. (1982). *Vulnerable but invincible: A study of resilient children.* New York: McGraw-Hill.

Wilcox, B., & Bellamy, G. T. (1987). *The catalogue.* Baltimore: Paul Brookes.

Wilkins, J. L. (1970). Producing suicides. *American Behavioral Scientist, 14*(2), 185–201.

Williams, J. M. (1984). *The psychological treatment of depression.* New York: The Free Press.

Willings, D., & Arsenault, M. (1986). Attempted suicide and creative promise. *Gifted Education International, 4*(1), 10–13.

Winn, D., & Halla, R. (1966). Observations of children who threaten to kill themselves. *Canadian Psychiatric Association, 11,* 283–294.

Wolfgang, M. E. (1958). *Patterns in criminal homicide.* Philadephia: University of Pennsylvania Press.

Wolfgang, M. E. (1959). Suicide by means of victim-precipitated homicide. *Journal of Clinical and Experimental Psychopathology, 20,* 335.

Youth suicide increases in Canada. (1985, June). *St. Petersburg Times,* p. 18A.

Zeitlin, A. (1985, February 7). Psychologist warns meeting of teen "suicide epidemic." *Gannett Westchester Newspapers,* p. 1.

Zeleny, L. D. (1983). Feeblemindedness in criminal conduct. *American Journal of Sociology, 139,* 564–576.

Index